JUN 1 1 2012

W9-BSS-975

PROPERTY OF
BOURBONNAIS PUBLIC LIBRARY

At Issue

| Standardized Testing

Other Books in the At Issue Series:

At Issue

| Standardized Testing

Dedria Bryfonski, Book Editor

GREENHAVEN PRESS
A part of Gale, Cengage Learning

GALE
CENGAGE Learning

Detroit • New York • San Francisco • New Haven, Conn • Waterville, Maine • London

371.26
STA

Elizabeth Des Chenes, *Managing Editor*

© 2012 Greenhaven Press, a part of Gale, Cengage Learning.

Gale and Greenhaven Press are registered trademarks used herein under license.

For more information, contact:
Greenhaven Press
27500 Drake Rd.
Farmington Hills, MI 48331-3535
Or you can visit our Internet site at gale.cengage.com

ALL RIGHTS RESERVED.
No part of this work covered by the copyright herein may be reproduced, transmitted, stored, or used in any form or by any means graphic, electronic, or mechanical, including but not limited to photocopying, recording, scanning, digitizing, taping, Web distribution, information networks, or information storage and retrieval systems, except as permitted under Section 107 or 108 of the 1976 United States Copyright Act, without the prior written permission of the publisher.

For product information and technology assistance, contact us at

Gale Customer Support, 1-800-877-4253
For permission to use material from this text or product, submit all requests online at www.cengage.com/permissions.

Further permissions questions can be e-mailed to permissionrequest@cengage.com.

Articles in Greenhaven Press anthologies are often edited for length to meet page requirements. In addition, original titles of these works are changed to clearly present the main thesis and to explicitly indicate the author's opinion. Every effort is made to ensure that Greenhaven Press accurately reflects the original intent of the authors. Every effort has been made to trace the owners of copyrighted material.

Cover image copyright © Todd Davidson/Illustration Works/Corbis.

LIBRARY OF CONGRESS CATALOGING-IN-PUBLICATION DATA

Standardized Testing / Dedria Bryfonski, book editor.
   p. cm. -- (At issue)
Summary: "Standardized Testing: Books in this anthology series focus a wide range of viewpoints onto a single controversial issue, providing in-depth discussions by leading advocates, a quick grounding in the issues, and a challenge to critical thinking skills"-- Provided by publisher.
   Includes bibliographical references and index.
   ISBN 978-0-7377-5598-5 (hardback) -- ISBN 978-0-7377-5599-2 (paperback)
   1. Educational tests and measurements--United States--Juvenile literature. I. Bryfonski, Dedria.
   LB3051.S7874 2012
   371.260973--dc23
                                                        2011044642

Printed in the United States of America
1 2 3 4 5 6 7 16 15 14 13 12

Contents

Introduction

Most historians trace the beginning of standardized testing to seventh-century China, when the government began administering written exams to select candidates for the civil service. As part of this exam, applicants were required to display a knowledge of Confucian philosophy and to compose poetry. Strenuous testing continues today in China with the Chinese National Higher Education Entrance Examinations, commonly called the Gaokao, or high test. The Gaokao is required to gain admittance to higher education in China. In 2010, ten million Chinese students took this test, competing for 5.7 million college and university placements. Manuela Zoninsein opines in *Slate*, "It is China's SAT—if the SAT lasted two days, covered everything learned since kindergarten, and had the power to determine one's entire professional trajectory."[1]

Standardized testing in the United States has a much shorter history. In 1845, public education advocate Horace Mann called for standardized testing of spelling, geography, and math in public schools. The impacts of immigration and the Industrial Revolution meant that schools were taking in a large influx of students, and standardized testing was adopted to more swiftly assess these students' abilities. In 1905, French psychologist Alfred Binet developed the first intelligence test, which was used by the military during World War I to assign soldiers to jobs.

The College Entrance Examination Board, now known as the College Board, was founded in the United States in 1900. It was initially an essay-based exam testing students in math, science, literature, and Latin. In 1926, in the interests of speed of testing and evaluation, the multiple-choice Scholastic Aptitude Test (SAT) was introduced.

Over succeeding decades, the results of US standardized tests have set off alarms. In 1957, the launch of Sputnik, the Soviet space satellite, raised the concern that US schools had fallen behind Soviet schools in science education. Prior to this time, standardized testing had been used to classify students. With the concern that US schools were trailing their Soviet counterparts, standardized testing began to be used to classify schools. In the mid-1970s, the College Board revealed that average SAT scores had been falling since 1963, an announcement that resulted in increased importance placed on testing. Then, in 1983, a national commission declared in the report "A Nation at Risk" that student achievement was declining, based on average SAT test scores. The backlash caused by this report resulted in even more emphasis on standardized testing.

In 2002, President George W. Bush signed into law the No Child Left Behind Act, mandating annual tests for all public school students. Under the law, schools are required to show adequate yearly progress on test scores, or they will be labeled as needing improvement. Such schools may face sanctions such as allowing students to transfer to another school or providing students free tutoring. If a school fails to show adequate yearly progress for four years in a row, it is labeled as needing corrective action and can face the wholesale replacement of its staff.

In December 2010, a furor arose when the Program for International Student Assessment (PISA) released the results of its test of nearly one-half million fifteen-year-olds worldwide in math, literacy, and science. This was the first year China participated in this test, and its students came in first in all three categories. By contrast, out of sixty-five countries, the United States ranked fourteenth in reading, seventeenth in science, and twenty-fifth in math. Although acknowledging that the participating students were from only one part of

China, the high-performing Shanghai province, many US educators said these results were cause for concern.

"This is an absolute wake-up call for America," US Education Secretary Arne Duncan said in an interview with the Associated Press. He added, "The results are extraordinarily challenging to us and we have to deal with the brutal truth. We have to get much more serious about investing in education."[2]

Echoing Duncan's concern was educator Charles Finn:

"Fifty-three years after Sputnik caused an earthquake in American education by giving us reason to believe that the Soviet Union had surpassed us, China has delivered another shock. On math, reading and science tests given to 15-year-olds in 65 countries last year, Shanghai's teenagers topped every other jurisdiction in all three subjects. Hong Kong also ranked in the top four on all three assessments. . . .

We must face the fact that China is bent on surpassing us, and everyone else, in education.

Will this news be the wake-up call that America needs to get serious about educational achievement? Will it get us beyond excuse-making, bickering over who should do what, and prioritizing adults over children?"[3]

Other educators and pundits urged not reading too much into these test scores. James Fallows, writing in the *Atlantic*, cautioned, "Take this seriously, and recognize that China is moving ahead in many, many ways. But recognize the fallibilities in this study, and don't go nuts."[4] Kam Wing Chan, professor in geography at the University of Washington, argued:

"The winner of the next true 'Sputnik race' will not be called by PISA test scores.

It will be decided, instead, by other strengths the US still has over China. . . .

US education is generally far broader than simply getting good test scores, while top Chinese schools fixate on those.

Kids in many American schools are exposed to a wider, sometimes open-ended, learning experience and are encouraged to explore beyond the conventional.

It is the openness and creativity of the American system and the opportunities it brings—the crucial factors that unleash the Bill Gateses of the world—that not only determine who eats the lunch but even what's on the menu."[5]

Whether the disparity between Chinese and US students on the PISA exam is cause for concern is just one of the numerous issues that surround the standardized testing controversy. In *At Issue: Standardized Testing*, educators, journalists, and commentators debate the validity of today's standardized tests as accurate, fair, and reliable measures of achievement and whether or not they have a justifiable place in the US educational system.

Notes

1. Manuela Zoninsein, "China's SAT," *Slate*, June 4, 2008.
2. The Associated Press, "In Ranking, U.S. Students Trail Global Leaders," *USA Today*, December 7, 2010.
3. Chester E. Finn Jr., "A Sputnik Moment for U.S. Education," *The Wall Street Journal*, December 8, 2010.
4. James Fallows, "On Those 'Stunning' Shanghai Test Scores," *The Atlantic*, December 7, 2010.
5. Kam Wing Chan, "Despite Recent Test Scores, China Is Not 'Eating Our Lunch,'" *The Seattle Times*, January 2, 2011.

1

Standardized Tests Effectively Measure Student Achievement

Herbert J. Walberg

Herbert J. Walberg, a distinguished visiting fellow at the Hoover Institution and a member of the Koret Task Force on K-12 Education, taught for thirty-five years at Harvard University and the University of Illinois at Chicago. He has authored or edited more than sixty books on education, including Tests, Testing, and Genuine School Reform, *on which this viewpoint is based.*

Standardized tests fairly and comprehensively measure student performance, thus directly benefiting students while holding teachers accountable. Students who study for a standardized test are more likely to complete their homework and watch less television than their peers. Thus, standardized test-taking develops habits that help students not only with the test but throughout life. While some teachers oppose standardized tests, most of their objections can be overcome through better test design and professional development programs.

President Barack Obama and leaders of the teachers' unions disagree with the view of citizens that schools, educators, and students should be held accountable for their performance on standardized tests. Despite strong public support for testing programs, influential educators have defined standardized tests as beasts that should be removed from schools. To quote one prominent critic, Gerald Bracey, they are "infer-

Herbert J. Walberg, "Stop the War Against Standardized Tests," *Defining Ideas: A Hoover Institution Journal*, May 20, 2011. Copyright © 2011 by The Hoover Institution. All rights reserved. Reproduced by permission.

nal machines of social destruction." Political leaders have also revealed a deep misunderstanding about the purpose and use of standardized testing when they claim tests are too simple or too biased to measure up to the subjective judgments of educators themselves. Such claims are naïve or deliberately misleading.

Student performance is a crucial element of a metaphorical three-legged stool that also includes standards and learning.

Good Measures of Student Performance

Research and experience show that standardized tests are generally good at measuring students' knowledge, skills, and understanding because they are objective, fair, efficient, and comprehensive. For these reasons, they are used for decisions about admission to colleges, graduate programs, and professional schools as well as qualification and licensing for many skilled occupations and demanding professions such as law and medicine. Given the misleading information and expressed views of some politicians and union leaders, it is worthwhile to review here the more specific reasons for using standardized tests.

Student performance is a crucial element of a metaphorical three-legged stool that also includes standards and learning. When one leg is weak or missing, educational programs may be faulty, but if all three are strong, the programs can be strong. Standardized tests are used to measure the student performance leg of this stool.

If standardized tests are misused, of course, the program and student learning may be defective. When standardized tests are used appropriately, a great deal can be learned about how well schools function. That information allows educators and policymakers to make better-informed conclusions about how much students are learning, which in turn allows them to make better-informed decisions about improving programs.

Targeting Areas for Development

Students benefit directly when they take tests that offer information on how well they have mastered the material intended for learning. School reading and mathematics skills, for example, can be precisely specified and as students learn the skills, they benefit from ongoing information tailored to their specific individual progress. Computers streamline this process by providing immediate feedback about correct and incorrect responses far more quickly and with much greater patience than teachers and tutors can provide.

Other general skills can also be both taught and measured. Writing, for example, can be subdivided into rules of spelling and grammar as well as skills of organization and style. As students improve their writing, they benefit from quick, objective feedback that helps them assess their specific progress on each skill and sub-skill.

Educators can better help students when they know how a student's objective performance compares with others. It helps both educators and students if students discover their strengths and weaknesses. For instance, performance information helps identify weaknesses that might be improved with tutoring and diligent study. Strengths revealed by standardized tests can help identify notable talents to be further developed in college study and in specialized vocations.

The costs of tests are less than 0.1 percent of total spending on K-12 education.

Standardized tests can provide such information at low costs and very little class time. Caroline Hoxby of Stanford University's Department of Economics and the Hoover Institution has estimated that that the costs of tests are less than

0.1 percent of total spending on K-12 education and amount to an average of less than $6 per student. A 50-item standardized test can be given in an hour or so and sample students' knowledge, understanding, and skills far more comprehensively than an essay test with only a few questions that can be answered in the same amount of time. This is not to say that students need no practice in writing, but such practice is better as a classroom exercise, a homework activity, or a term paper rather than an objective assessment of the many aspects of learning.

Encouraging Learning

Comparative studies by John Bishop of Cornell University provide evidence of the learning value of standardized tests. In one study, he found that countries requiring students to take nationally standardized tests showed higher test scores on international tests than those in countries not requiring such tests.

In a second study, Bishop found that U.S. students who anticipated having to pass a standardized test for high school graduation learned more science and math, were more likely to complete homework and talk with their parents about schoolwork, and watched less television than their peers who were not required to pass such exams. These constructive activities encourage students to concentrate on meeting standards and monitoring their own time and progress—skills important for not only increased achievement but also increased success in life.

Still, there are those who oppose standardized tests for a variety of reasons.

Objections Are Easily Countered

Those who argue against standardized tests say that holding educators and students accountable for only mathematics and reading encourages them to neglect history and science. But this is an argument for comprehensive and systematic testing across the entire curriculum, not an argument against standardized tests themselves.

Responsible test-makers, moreover, do not purport to cover all the material the students are expected to learn. Tests sample only a small fraction, perhaps as little as 5 to 10 percent, of all content and skills—just as a national survey may interview as few as 1,500 people for an estimate, within a few percentage points, of national attitudes. Like a national survey that samples the major parts of the country, a standardized test can sample the multiple topics students are expected to learn.

Those who oppose standardized tests also argue that the tests can only measure simple facts that can be memorized. But tests assessing advanced understanding and judgment do exist. They may, for instance, require respondents to select the best idea from a group of different and compelling positions. They may require respondents to identify the best reason for action, the best interpretation of a set of ideas, or the best application of important principles. (Rather than the word "correct," the word "best" is often used because more than one answer may be correct to some degree, but only one is best.)

Helping American Students Be More Globally Competitive

K-12 students who practice demonstrating their knowledge and skills on standardized tests throughout their school career become better prepared to meet future educational, occupational, and professional goals. They will be ready for the standardized tests assessing complex achievement that are used for admission to selective colleges and graduate and professional schools. In addition, K-12 students will be prepared for tests required for occupational licensing for trades as well as for intellectually demanding professions such as law and medicine. The American Board of Internal Medicine, for example, uses multiple-choice, standardized tests to assess a physician's judgment before he can be certified in an advanced medical specialty.

Another complaint against standardized tests is that they cause stress among educators and students. But the world outside of school is demanding. Indeed, the knowledge economy increasingly demands more knowledge and better skills from workers, which require larger amounts of intense study of difficult subjects. Yet American students spend only about half the total study time that Asian students do in regular schools, in tutoring schools, and in homework, a major reason for their poor performance relative to Asian and European students in international surveys. Thus, some reasonable pressure and objective performance measurements are advisable for the future welfare of the students and the nation.

Good student performance on tests should be a source of satisfaction among successful educators.

When students can see their progress toward attaining standards, moreover, undue pressure can be mitigated and their incremental progress may motivate them. As in games and sports, practice and accountability can enhance performance. Just as difficulty levels established in recreational activities are common, testing programs allow educators to accommodate their curriculum to better meet the needs of students with different achievement levels. Teachers can use test results to identify and respond directly to the specific needs of individual students by giving special help to those who fall behind and accelerating or enriching learning for advanced students.

Taking Pride in Student Achievement

Finally, some critics of testing complain that tests cause educators malaise. But good schools focus on student learning, not on the satisfaction of the professional staff. If the data show that testing benefits students, it should be pursued even if there isn't unanimous teacher support. Professionals should take pride in seeing good results from their work, and because testing reveals good work and aids rather than detracts from instruction, teachers should embrace it and even get paid for the good performance of their students.

Much of teacher dissatisfaction with testing is attributable to a lack of familiarity with why testing is necessary and how good tests are designed and administered. Often, a particular teacher's opposition is based on a past experience in which a test was poorly designed, not aligned with the curriculum, or incorrectly administered. Professional development programs that include guidance on how to align classroom activities with achievement standards can address these problems. In one study, teachers were able to see the shortcomings of tests they designed and, thus, learned how to devise better tests. As a result, the teachers also gained respect for standardized tests designed by testing specialists.

Good student performance on tests should be a source of satisfaction among successful educators. The appropriate tests can reveal strengths and weaknesses in the curriculum and instruction. Our nation's poor achievement progress shows that substantial improvements in teaching and learning are needed—and progress on those two fronts can and should be measured by standardized tests.

2

Standardized Tests Do Not Effectively Measure Student Achievement

Phillip Harris, Bruce M. Smith, and Joan Harris

Phillip Harris is executive director of the Association for Educational Communications & Technology. For twenty-seven years, Bruce M. Smith was a member of the editorial staff of the Phi Delta Kappan, *the flagship publication of Phi Delta Kappa International, the association for professional educators. He retired as editor-in-chief in 2008. Joan Harris has taught first, second, and third grades for more than twenty-five years. In 1997, she was recognized by the National Association for the Education of Young Children as the outstanding teacher of the year.*

Contrary to popular assumptions about standardized testing, the tests do a poor job of measuring student achievement. They fail to measure such important attributes as creativity and critical thinking skills. Studies indicate that standardized tests reward superficial thinking and may discourage more analytical thinking. Additionally, because of the small sample of knowledge that is tested, standardized tests provide a very incomplete picture of student achievement.

Despite what reports in your local newspaper suggest, scores of standardized tests are *not* the same as student achievement. What's more, the scores don't provide very much

Phillip Harris, Bruce M. Smith, and Joan Harris, "Chapter 3: The Tests Don't Measure Achievement Adequately," *The Myths of Standardized Tests: Why They Don't Tell You What You Think They Do*, 2011, pp. 33–45. Copyright © 2011 by Rowman & Littlefield Publishers. All rights reserved. Reproduced by permission.

useful information for evaluating a student's achievement, a teacher's competency, or the success of a particular school or program. To make such judgments, you need to move beyond the scores themselves and make some inferences about what they might mean. . . .

The assumption underlying standardized testing . . . is: *When we want to understand student achievement, it is enough to talk about scores on standardized tests.* Accepting this assumption at face value, as nearly all journalists, pundits, and politicians do, is to fall prey to a "dangerous illusion."

"Achievement" means more than a score on a standardized test.

How to Define "Achievement"

Let's start with the question of defining achievement. If someone asked you to say in your own words exactly what is meant by "student achievement," how would you respond? If you said student achievement is what's measured by the state achievement tests, it's time to look a little harder at what these tests actually can and cannot do. More than a decade ago, education economist Richard Rothstein stated the problem directly: "Measurement of student achievement is complex—too complex for the social science methods presently available." And those methods certainly included standardized testing.

That was 1998, but the passage of more than a decade hasn't made it easier to evaluate student achievement in any systematic way, especially in a way that will yield the kind of numbers you can spread out along an axis to make comparisons. If anything, the intervening years—primarily the years of No Child Left Behind (NCLB) and its strict test-driven regimen—have made the problems in this area worse because we've asked test scores to carry ever more weight and we've depended on them to make ever more consequential decisions. Because of NCLB—and the [Barack] Obama administration's "blueprint" places similar weight on test scores—we now use "achievement test" scores to decide whether students are entitled to tutoring services or whether they can transfer to a different school or whether we should close a school and reconstitute its staff. And many states now have strict rules about who qualifies to receive a high school diploma primarily by the scores on a standardized test of "achievement."

But "achievement" means more than a score on a standardized test. We knew it in 1998, and we know it now. For instance, as part of a larger project to ensure equity in math classrooms, the National Council of Teachers of Mathematics (NCTM), a group whose members are not strangers to the use of numerical data and statistical interpretation, reminded its members of some terms and definitions that would be important in the larger equity project. Rochelle Gutiérrez and her colleagues offered readers of the *NCTM News Bulletin* the following description of an appropriate understanding of "achievement": "Achievement—all the outcomes that students and teachers attain. Achievement is more than test scores but also includes class participation, students' course-taking patterns, and teachers' professional development patterns." The standardized tests we all know so well don't even come close to assessing all the outcomes that students and teachers attain.

Many Attributes Cannot Be Measured

As psychometrician Daniel Koretz puts it, scores on a standardized test "usually do not provide a direct and complete measure of educational achievement." He cites two reasons why this is so, and both are related to our earlier discussion of sampling. First, tests can measure only a portion of the *goals* of education, which are necessarily broader and more inclusive than the test could possibly be. . . . Here is Gerald Bracey's list of some of the biggies that we generally don't even try to use standardized tests to measure:

creativity

critical thinking

resilience

motivation

persistence

curiosity

endurance

reliability

enthusiasm

empathy

self-awareness

self-discipline

leadership

civic-mindedness

courage

compassion

resourcefulness

sense of beauty

sense of wonder

honesty

integrity

Surely these are attributes we all want our children to acquire in some degree. And while not all learning takes place in classrooms, these are real and valuable "achievements." Shouldn't schools pursue goals such as these for their students, along with the usual academic goals? Of course, a teacher can't really teach all of these things from a textbook. But, as Bracey points out, she can model them or talk with students about people who exemplify them. But she has to have enough time left over to do so after getting the kids ready for the standardized test of "achievement."

Standardized tests inadvertently create incentives for students to become superficial thinkers.

A Reward for Shallow Thinking

In fact, there are more problems associated with the impact of standardized testing on "achievement" than simply the fact that the technology of the testing cannot efficiently and accurately measure some vitally important attributes that we all want our children to "achieve." Alfie Kohn put it this way:

> Studies of students of different ages have found *a statistical association between students with high scores on standardized tests and relatively shallow thinking.* One of these studies classified elementary school students as "actively engaged if they went back over things they didn't understand, asked questions of themselves as they read, and tried to connect what they were doing to what they had already learned; and as 'superficially' engaged if they just copied down answers, guessed a lot, and skipped the hard parts. It turned out that the superficial style was positively correlated with high scores on the Comprehensive Test of Basic Skills (CTBS) and Metropolitan Achievement Test (MAT). Similar findings have emerged from studies of middle school and high school students."(Emphasis in original.)

So by ignoring attributes that they can't properly assess, standardized tests inadvertently create incentives for students to become superficial thinkers—to seek the quick, easy, and obvious answer. That's hardly an "achievement" that most parents want for their children. And surely it's not what our policy makers and education officials hope to achieve by incessantly harping on "achievement." In our view, most of these policy makers mean well, but when they say "achievement," they clearly mean test scores and only test scores. But to assume that the test scores can take the place of all the other information we need to know in order to have a good understanding of students' development leads us to some poor conclusions about how our children are growing physically, emotionally, and intellectually. The information provided by test scores is very limited, and consequently we must be very careful in drawing inferences about what the scores mean.

Measuring Only Small Samples

The second reason Koretz cites for the incompleteness of test scores as a measure of achievement [is as follows]: "Even in assessing the goals that can be measured well, tests are generally very small samples of behavior that we use to make estimates of students' mastery of very large domains of knowledge and skill." So apart from not doing a very good job of measuring achievement in such areas as creativity or persistence, standardized tests have another serious limitation: whenever a small part of a domain is made to stand in for the larger whole, we must be very careful about the inferences we draw from the data we obtain.

3

Standardized Testing Encourages Teachers to Be Creative

Stuart Buck, Nathan C. Jensen, Gary W. Ritter, and Caleb P. Rose

Stuart Buck, Nathan C. Jensen, and Caleb P. Rose are research associates and Gary W. Ritter is a professor of education policy at the College of Education and Health Professions, University of Arkansas.

A review of education literature reveals that articles critical of standardized testing outweigh positive articles by a nine-to-one margin. To better understand teachers' attitudes toward testing, the authors interviewed forty-two teachers in five Arkansas schools in 2009. While the teachers initially complained about standardized tests, most of them concluded that the tests helped them to be more creative and collaborative. Additionally, they welcomed the accountability and the data that the tests provided about their students.

It's hard to know what teachers really think about testing. On the one hand, teachers are constantly giving tests and quizzes and morning work and a myriad of assessments to ensure that the students are following along and understand-

Stuart Buck, Nathan C. Jensen, Gary W. Ritter, and Caleb P. Rose, "Teachers Say the Most Interesting Things—An Alternative View of Testing: In Spite of the Barrage of Anti-Testing News, Some Teachers Say Tests Have Not Sapped Their Creativity or Hindered Collaboration and That They Appreciate Having Useful Data, a Road Map for Instruction, a Sense of Accountability for All Educators," *Phi Delta Kappan*, March 2010, ed 6, vol 91, page 50. Copyright © 2010 by Phi Delta Kappan International. All rights reserved. Reproduced by permission.

ing the material. Presumably, the teachers believe in the importance of monitoring student progress on a very regular basis, and testing is one tool that teachers employ to do this.

A Paradoxical View of Testing

On the other hand, there's a widespread belief that teachers as a group oppose more standardized testing. Indeed, in the age of No Child Left Behind (NCLB), numerous commentators have criticized testing for forcing teachers to abandon creative lesson plans in exchange for the dreary process of rote memorization and prepping for multiple-choice tests. During his transition into office, even President [Barack] Obama agreed with these criticisms by stating on his change.gov web site that "teachers should not be forced to spend the academic year preparing students to fill in bubbles on standardized tests." We checked the education literature and found further evidence that educators and faculty in schools of education are resistant to standardized testing. In a cursory review of three policy-oriented education journals (*Educational Researcher*, *Educational Leadership*, and *Phi Delta Kappan*) over the past five years, we found that articles critical to testing outnumbered the favorable articles by an overwhelming 9-to-1 ratio.

Thus, the attitude of teachers toward testing is somewhat puzzling—this is a group that uses testing regularly but is concerned about the potential pitfalls of assessment-based reform. Indeed, it's not clear why testing and standards would inherently cause poor teaching. After all, if a state's standards include the skills that students are required to learn, and if that state's test covers a fair sample of those standards, then teachers will teach the skills that students need to learn. Testing should not hinder good teachers from teaching these skills, whatever they are, in a creative and an intellectually curious manner.

To gain a better understanding of this interesting paradox, we decided to talk to some local teachers to get their views on "teaching to the test." In spring 2009, our team of researchers interviewed 42 teachers in five Arkansas schools to study how testing influenced their classroom instruction. We didn't go into this blind; this was the end of "testing season," and we expected to find, at best, some staunch critics of testing and, at worst, some angry educators.

The State Context in Arkansas

As is the case in many other states, Arkansas students in grades 3–8 take weeklong, criterion-referenced, benchmark tests. The Arkansas criterion-referenced test items are combined with items from the norm-referenced Stanford Achievement Test, 10th Edition (SAT-10) into one "augmented" set of annual exams. Moreover, high school students in Arkansas take end-of-course exams in algebra, geometry, literacy, and biology, which are also closely aligned with Arkansas' Curriculum Frameworks.

To gather the views of these educators, we conducted focus groups with teachers and principals in five schools in three medium-sized Arkansas school districts. The focus groups lasted for about an hour at each school, with about 8–10 teachers (and occasionally principals) present for each interview. During these sessions, we guided the discussions around central questions, such as whether teachers found the Arkansas benchmark tests helpful, whether they thought testing prevented them from teaching creatively, whether classroom hours became focused on test prep rather than learning, and what they thought of the concept of "teaching to the test." Broadly stated, we simply wanted to know how the existence of the Arkansas state exams influenced teaching and learning in teachers' classrooms.

What the Teachers Said

Because our focus groups were conducted just days after the end of the spring exam period, we wouldn't have been surprised if the sessions became venting sessions for exhausted teachers with nothing good to say about testing. At first, the teachers didn't disappoint; most sessions opened with a list of criticisms of the state's standardized testing regime. Some teachers voiced the usual complaints that testing is too focused on bubbling in answers, that testing isn't conducive to the strengths of more "active" learners, and that the tests are too "knowledge-based" and "multiple-choice." Other teachers said the testing period could be shortened so as not to exhaust the students. Still others maintained that testing should measure academic growth rather than absolute levels of attainment. Of course, these results are predictable and not all that interesting.

What happened next was the interesting part. After the surprisingly short introductory period in which teachers voiced complaints, teachers began talking about good aspects of the Arkansas exams. One teacher followed the other, with no prompting from the researchers leading the focus groups. In the end, teachers said many good things about various aspects of the testing process and, overall, gave a very positive impression of the effects of the annual assessments on classroom teaching. After we sifted through all of the comments from all of the teachers at all of the school sites, five positive themes emerged. The consensus of teachers with whom we spoke was that the tests provide useful data, that the testing regime helps create a road map for the year's instruction, that the standards and tests don't sap creativity or hinder collaboration, and, perhaps most surprising, that the accountability imposed by the testing regime is useful.

Tests Provide Useful Data

Theme #1: Tests provide useful data. Almost all teachers agreed that tests provide useful data showing whether students have grasped certain concepts. As one teacher put it, "I do think it has been very helpful in our building for when they walk in on day one to know this kid really doesn't know this, this kid didn't understand . . . and that data has certainly helped us to know our kids much better." Another teacher said, "as soon as we get our class lists, we'll have those results too . . . I actually sat down with my kids and said, 'OK, this is where we were messing up.'" Indeed, these comments exemplify a belief shared by many proponents and opponents of testing—more data is one clearly positive outcome of the recent emphasis on student testing.

Almost all teachers agreed that tests provide useful data showing whether students have grasped certain concepts.

Theme #2: Testing and standards help create a road map for the year's instruction. Many teachers noted that before testing, it was easy to teach idiosyncratically—perhaps spending "six weeks on the dinosaur unit and just totally ignor-[ing]" other topics. With increased focus on testing, however, teachers have focused on matching their instruction to a coherent set of standards. Thus, one math teacher said that while she had initially "hated" the Arkansas benchmark tests, she has since changed her mind: "I'm OK with it now, to be honest; I see where knowing the standards and knowing what's going to be tested can help me plan the whole year and make sure I've covered everything." One additional benefit of standardization—a "lifesaver," as one teacher put it—is that districts can collaborate in setting a consistent schedule for teaching the state standards, which means that "if a child moves from [neighboring town] to our school . . . they should be right where we are."

This point assumes that a state's tests are aligned with the state's curricular standards; without such alignment, schools would face conflicting signals and would therefore have a difficult time creating a consistent road map. Most teachers agreed that the Arkansas tests do a fairly good job of matching the Arkansas standards. This finding is also in line with an argument made by many advocates for testing and standards— that standards foster clarity about what should be taught each year.

Testing Does Not Discourage Creativity

Theme #3: Test-prep does not necessarily sap creativity, for teachers or students. Several teachers disagreed with the notion that testing forces teachers to replace creative lessons with dreary test-prep. One math teacher said, "I used to think and really had a strong opinion that it caused me not to be a creative teacher, but I've changed now." Another teacher—one who was often critical of testing—said that "true creative people" will "find a way to be creative regardless of what the framework is." When asked if tests discourage creativity, one teacher claimed that "I think it's done just the opposite . . . I think adding open response where you used to have tests that were just strictly multiple-choice has forced teachers to be more creative." From another school, a teacher said, "In science and math, we're expected to use manipulatives as much as possible and do hands-on as much as possible . . . I do so much more now, so much more."

Test-prep does not necessarily sap creativity, for teachers or students.

As such, many teachers praised the Arkansas tests for encouraging more creative and critical thinking by students. Due to the many open-response questions in math and English, students "have to understand it [the material] to get the points on that [test]; they can't just make a guess and maybe get it right." One teacher remarked that "as an older teacher," the introduction of benchmarks and tests "totally changed the way we taught because [formerly] we were just answering questions; we didn't have them think about, 'why is this the answer?'" In this way, the Arkansas tests encourage both teachers and students to be creative and to think more deeply about questions and answers.

We were certainly surprised to find that teachers voicing the "testing prevents creativity" criticism were distinctly in the minority. One teacher in particular summed up the opinions of many other teachers: "I think that [if] there's somebody who says, 'Oh all you do is teach to the test and you're not being very creative,' I think they haven't been in the classroom in a long time—either that or they've been in a classroom or a school where their principal is not doing their job." In other words, whether testing saps creativity depends on the teachers and principals. They could respond to the perceived pressure by resorting to dull lessons premised on rote memorization, but they could also seek creative strategies for ensuring student learning. For many teachers in our Arkansas sample, the testing regime fostered greater creativity.

Testing Aids Collaboration

Theme #4: Testing can lead to collaboration. Many teachers claimed that the Arkansas exams encouraged teacher collaboration to ensure that students are well-prepared. As one teacher said, testing "does give us a common goal, and we can work together." From a different school, a teacher asserted that "I feel like we have a lot more open policy teacher-to-teacher now because everybody's reaching for the best way. . . . It's just so worth it to collaborate with your other teachers on better ideas and seeing what they do that you can do better."

Teachers at one school had adopted a professional learning community (PLC) model. Several teachers in that school said that they used to hate testing, but that they now thought testing had introduced a greater sense of collaboration in ensuring that each child learned everything that he or she was supposed to know. Teachers at the PLC school reported that they regularly gathered to decide on the "eight to 10 essential standards and try to focus on just those." Most teachers rose to the challenge that the testing provided by teaming together to enhance student achievement.

Teachers Welcome Accountability

Theme #5: Accountability is useful. This final theme was the most surprising because many criticisms of testing are related to the accountability that comes with the exams. That is, while many educators welcome the data and information that standardized assessments provide, few will claim an affinity for the consequences that are sometimes attached to student performance on these tests. Nevertheless, teachers in our focus groups even made positive comments that the testing programs encourage teachers to feel an even greater responsibility that students learn the material.

Accountability is useful.

One teacher noted that tests "hold accountable" those teachers who "are just there to get summers off and an 8-to-3 job." From another school, a teacher said: "We all need accountability. . . . [It] helps us be better teachers and not just take a day off because we don't feel like it and let [the students] watch a movie." At a third school, a teacher said, "I absolutely believe in accountability and having [the students] know those benchmarks before they go on to another grade." And from a fourth school, a teacher pointed out that "the only way someone might say [that testing makes teaching] less desirable is because they're [teachers] going to work harder."

As a specific example of how testing encourages teachers to be accountable for ensuring that each student makes progress, one teacher noted that "I've totally changed my philosophy of teaching. I used to stand up there and teach the best of my knowledge, and if they didn't get it, 'Sorry, we've got to move on.' But now it's, 'OK, these kids didn't learn it;

what's the plan?'" These teachers used to hold themselves accountable for delivering good lessons; now, thanks to the testing regime, the teachers can go one step further by assessing whether the lessons translated into improved student learning.

Testing Spurs Creativity in Teachers

Before we walked into the schools, we anticipated a chorus of complaints confirming that testing, in and of itself, is a negative force, as is argued in some 90% of the literature we examined. What we found was surprising: While some teachers criticize testing for inhibiting creativity, most maintained that testing and standards spurred their creativity. Further, while one teacher claimed that she had to race through all of the Arkansas standards to be sure that everything was covered by the test date and that she had to abandon her former attitude of "stick with it until they got it," more teachers said that testing had forced them to make sure that every child understood the lessons.

One important limitation was that teachers in our focus groups were not serving in extraordinarily low-achieving schools. While these educators were well aware of AYP (Adequate Yearly Progress) and were concerned about their schools being on or near alert status, they did not work in schools that were under constant accountability pressure from day one. Thus, teachers in such low-achieving schools could feel different pressure from the testing system and view the influence of testing quite differently than do the teachers in our sample.

Nonetheless, these teachers work each day in typical American schools, with good but not great student performance. Their opinions are not generalizable to all teachers across the country, but we also suspect that we didn't manage to stumble upon the only teachers in the country who see benefits of student testing.

In the end, if some teachers and principals believe testing has changed their pedagogical approaches for the worse, they might be able to gain some insight from other teachers who are still able to present creative and interesting lessons and to concentrate on student learning, as we found in our focus groups. The existence of teachers who report that these tests actually add to the learning process suggests that standardized tests might not be the hindrance they're made out to be. Indeed, most teachers support the general concept of student assessment—they reveal this in their actions each day when they ask students to prepare for tests and quizzes and submit homework assignments. And the teachers in our sample demonstrated that, if they want to, they can use state standards and state exams to become even better educators through more data, coherence, creativity, collaboration, and even accountability.

4

Standards and Assessments Are Not Always Meaningful

Rob Montgomery

Rob Montgomery is an assistant professor of English education at Kennesaw State University in Georgia. He is a National Writing Project fellow specializing in pre-service English education, composition studies, and adolescent literacy.

Over a fifteen-year period, there has been a sea change in American education as education reform has resulted in a focus on content standards and standardized testing. Although testing, standards, and accountability, when applied correctly, can produce positive results, existing standards and tests are poorly constructed. As an example, in California's assessment system, the content standards are neither properly aligned with meaningful instruction nor accurately assessed.

In my nearly 15-year progression from teaching in a high school classroom to teaching future teachers in a university classroom, I've gained an unusual perspective on American education, one that led me to want to take stock of our current standards—and test-obsessed climate. In 1995, as I began my teaching career, I was blissfully ignorant of both content standards and high-stakes standardized testing. I received my initial teacher certification that year from the state of Ohio, one of the first states to institute a benchmark, high-stakes exit exam for its students.

Rob Montgomery, "Education: Standards and Assessments in Practice," *World and I Online*, February 2010, ed. 2, vol. 25, www.worldandijournal.com. Copyright © 2010 by World and I Online. All rights reserved. Reproduced by permission.

Few Guidelines for Teachers

My university methods class in English/Language Arts had taught me how to write a lesson plan, structure a novel unit, and respond to student writing. But even though the Ohio 9th Grade Exit Exam had been instituted three years before, there was no talk of standards, content or otherwise, and no discussion, as far as I can remember, of teaching to the test. When I compare my own teacher-training and student teaching experiences with the teaching and research I have conducted recently, I see so few similarities between them that it almost appears I was trained for an entirely different profession.

When I received my first job later in 1995, teaching 9th and 10th grade English in California, nothing had changed fundamentally from my training in the Midwest. I know now that California had a curriculum framework for English/Language Arts (E/LA) in place at that time (specifically, 1985's Model Curriculum Standards: Grades Nine Through Twelve), and this framework had grade level expectations for students, but I never would have guessed that from the materials handed to me at my new teacher orientation.

My department chair gave me two small binders, one for each grade level I was teaching. The 9th grade binder told me I would teach short stories, *To Kill a Mockingbird*, and *Romeo & Juliet*, and I was free to choose additional novels from the included reading list. Additionally, I was asked to teach a variety of literary terminology specific to prose (exposition, conflict, rising action, etc.), as well as the narrative essay.

My 10th grade binder looked much the same. I would teach poetry (and its related terminology), two core novels (*Lord of the Flies* and *Black Boy*), the persuasive essay, and the research paper. There was a general expectation in both grades to teach vocabulary and grammar, but no guidelines as to which words or concepts. That was the extent of the direction I was given as a 22-year-old teacher fresh off a plane from Ohio.

A Focus on Standards

Six years later, the world had changed. When I returned to the classroom after a one-year stint in graduate school, California had instituted their brand-new curriculum frameworks and content standards. I now had an expansive, state-mandated list of items to cover with my students, running the gamut from vocabulary acquisition to public speaking. Students were tested on these standards, and 10th grade students now had to pass an exit exam in order to receive their diploma. In my district, course outlines had to be rewritten showing how every aspect of every class related to the standards. We adopted a textbook anthology that provided teachers with discussion questions, worksheets, and tests all tied directly to California's content standards and we were encouraged to use these resources to ensure that we were meeting the standards.

Site administrators required teachers to conspicuously post the content standards that related to that day's lesson, and they were diligent in spot-checking classrooms to ensure that the standards were, in fact, posted. Department meetings, staff meetings, and staff development days focused not on how to better meet student needs, but on how to better meet the content standards and their accompanying tests, apparently assuming that these two very different goals were actually one and the same.

It is one thing ... to be in favor of accountability, and another thing entirely to see what this accountability looks like in practice.

As I became involved in teacher education working with pre-service teachers in E/LA at the graduate school level I saw that the emphasis on standards was not isolated to kindergarten through grade 12 education. I was required to instruct the student teachers in how to meet the content standards, and the students were asked to demonstrate this in their lesson planning. They were also asked to discuss the ways in which they met standards and objectives in their major teaching assessment, the Performance Assessment for California Teachers (PACT).

In the two years that I taught the Methods and Procedures course for the E/LA cohort, the student teachers reported that they felt pressure to meet the standards, and were constantly concerned that they were failing to live up to these state-mandated expectations. Additionally, no matter how successful they had become in developing their own lessons, most of the student teachers were required to shift gears completely in the weeks leading up to the spring standardized tests, abandoning literature and authentic writing assessments in lieu of isolated lessons on test preparation.

It is one thing, I have discovered, to be in favor of accountability, and another thing entirely to see what this accountability looks like in practice. For me, the school year would get hijacked once in March for the California High School Exit Exam (CAHSEE), and again in April for the series of Standardized Testing and Reporting (STAR) assessments. Spread over two weeks, the five days of STAR testing (covering the core content areas of English, Social Science, Science, and Mathematics) took up roughly half the school day, and required that the daily schedule be rearranged so that there would be some sort of equity in class meeting times. Predictably, the students were frazzled and exhausted after three to four hours of testing each day, so even though classes met for roughly the same amount of time, productivity was nearly zero. And, as with the CAHSEE, much time and energy was devoted to test preparation.

Students Do Not Take Some Tests Seriously

Additionally, teachers and administration had to come up with ways to get the students to take the test seriously. Unlike the CAHSEE, where graduation is contingent upon a passing score, there is no real reason for students to view the STAR as anything more than a hoop to jump through each spring. They are not punished for a poor performance, nor are they rewarded for an outstanding one. Hanging potential classification as a "Program Improvement" school over their heads isn't a credible or meaningful threat, and since the Governor's Scholarship program, which awarded top-performing students $1,000, lasted only three years, it is hard to find a good reason for students to expend effort on an assessment for which they receive nothing in return. In my observations, I've seen schools resort to various "carrots": offering a carnival during school hours for students who improved their scores over the previous year, extending lunch time, or awarding gift cards from various local businesses. It is unclear if this actually did anything to boost student performance.

Bearing all of this in mind the overhaul of school curricula, the implementation of new tests, the drastic changes required of administrators, teachers, and students by high-stakes tests one crucial question has been left unasked by many and unanswered altogether: are the standards and tests, in their present form, promoting student learning? If they are not, it casts serious doubt on whether all the time and energy expended so far has been worth it, and raises troubling questions about the schools that have already received punitive measures under the mandates of NCLB [No Child Left Behind].

Lack of Alignment with Meaningful Instruction

Troubled by the changes I witnessed as a result of my own teaching experiences, I spent three years researching California's system of standards and assessments. I focused on the twelve Literary Response and Analysis standards (the curricular tasks dealing with the study of literature) at the 9th and 10th grade level, analyzing them to determine just what they wanted students and teachers to know and be able to do with literature, and also examining the corresponding STAR test questions released by the state in an effort to see exactly what kind of knowledge of the standards was being measured.

As a result of this research (which also included interviews with practicing teachers), I worry that there is A) a disconnect between the content standards and what constitutes meaningful instruction in literature, and B) a lack of accuracy in the way the standards are assessed by the STAR.

My fear is that California's current system of standards and assessments might represent nothing more than an empty gesture toward increased intellectual rigor and higher standards for graduation, but is, in reality, a sort of pseudo-literacy that sounds impressive, but falls apart under genuine scrutiny.

A practical example would be helpful. In my analysis of the standards, I found that, among other things, the standards often misrepresent (or even misunderstand) the way readers make meaning of texts. Standard 3.5 asks that students "compare works that express a universal theme and provide evidence to support the ideas in each work." There are other problems with this standard, but most troublesome is the idea that texts "express" a theme. The implication of Standard 3.5 is that a student reads a text, and the theme immediately leaps from the pages, as though it were contained within and merely waiting to be released by the reader. This is a view of literature instruction with which many critics and well-informed teachers would disagree, as this approach seems to ignore the fact that not every student reads the same way, and therefore not all themes will exist equally for all students.

Louise Rosenblatt's transactional theory of reading, with its notion that students interact with a text based on their own history and experience, allows for individual interpretations of texts, and the possibility that not every child will arrive at the same thematic understanding. Looked at in this way, the theme isn't "expressed" by a text and received by a student; rather, the theme is arrived at after the student interacts with the text, applies his or her own knowledge, and arrives at an understanding. To put it another way, a theme isn't found in a text; theme is imposed on a text by the reader during the process of constructing meaning.

Even if we were to adopt this extremely flawed and reductive view of how people read, and remembering that Standard 3.5 apparently allows for only one theme to be discussed, who gets to choose which theme is the "right" theme? In Huckleberry Finn, I can see how there could be a wide range of themes at which a student might arrive in his reading. A student could plausibly believe the novel to be about any one (or more) of these themes: the evils of slavery; the need to avoid hypocrisy; the debilitating effect of racial injustice; the importance of friendship; the perils of growing up; finding redemption in the wilderness. Are any of these more worthy of discussion than the others? Who makes that decision? The teacher? The students? And on what are they basing their decision? Standard 3.5 doesn't see any of these issues as problematic, since apparently there is only one theme in a text, and you can find it there if only you look hard, enough.

A Failure to Understand Core Concepts

Ideally, the STAR test items that correspond with this standard would shed light on exactly what teachers should do with it. However, at the 9th grade level, the STAR does nothing to illuminate just what Standard 3.5 is after. In fact, it makes matters more difficult.

After reading two short texts (an excerpt from a prose passage about scuba diving, and a Noboa Polanco poem titled "Identity"), the students are asked to identify what "sense" is conveyed by each passage. This is, of course, not a question about theme. Asking students what sense they receive from a text indicates mood or tone. What it does not indicate is theme, in any way that I have ever taught the concept myself, or seen it taught by others.

This only reinforces my fear that the authors of the standards (and now, I see, the STAR) have themselves only a rudimentary knowledge of the concepts they have established as requisite student knowledge. How else to make sense of a test question supposedly assessing knowledge of theme that in fact has nothing whatsoever to do with theme? It is not entirely clear what the standard wants teachers to do, and this test question only serves to muddy the waters by implying that tone or mood are somehow comparable to theme.

> *The authors of the standards . . . have themselves only a rudimentary knowledge of the concepts they have established.*

It comes as a relief, then, that while I may not agree with the views embodied by the 10th grade questions, they at least possess a semblance of alignment with what I think the standard is asking of teachers and students. The problem, though, is that they do seem to adhere to the reductive view of reading and meaning-making that I believe Standard 3.5 embodies (that is, a single theme rests in the text and will be discovered by a competent reader). In two questions, students are asked to identify issues of theme dealing with two separate poems. In both cases, the questions make the assumption that students will read and arrive at the same theme as the test-makers. This ignores what we know about how readers read texts and make meaning of them, and is troublesome because a student could read the poems and understand them, but arrive at a different thematic interpretation than the one endorsed by the STAR.

The effect on the student, then, is that he believes his reading of the poems to be "wrong." This is the problem with asking questions about theme and meaning on multiple-choice tests. We know that there can be variances in interpretation, but standards and tests (or at least these standards and tests) act as if there is only one "right" answer, and if you don't agree with the test-makers, you will be penalized.

If we look to the test questions released by the state to clarify what is meant by each standard, here is what we can now conclude about Standard 3.5: At the 9th grade level, we learned that theme is roughly the same thing as tone and mood, and at the 10th grade level, we learned that theme is seen as singular and based on an authoritative reading of the text by a removed third party. For the released STAR test questions, only a third of them seemed to accurately assess the identified standard. In another third, I couldn't figure out what they were assessing. My position to standards and assessments is not adversarial, but it strikes me that these results are simply not acceptable.

Standards and Testing Only Add Bureaucracy

I have no problem with holding teachers and students to high standards, nor am I opposed to using some form of assessment to determine if they are meeting these standards. However, as I look back over the changes occurring in public education in the 15 years since I finished my teacher training, I don't see the current system of standards and assessments as accomplishing much more than adding an additional level of bureaucracy to our schools. More to the point, if the [Barack] Obama administration's rhetoric is anything to go by, standards and assessments are here to stay.

I don't see the current system of standards and assessments as accomplishing much more than adding an additional level of bureaucracy.

Common core standards are currently in development, and there is talk of increased accountability for teachers (with tenure contingent on students' satisfactory test performance) as well as teacher-training programs. It is absolutely vital, then, if we are to buy into this system, that we see the standards as reflecting meaningful instructional tasks, and the assessments as accurately and thoughtfully evaluating student performance on those standards. For over a decade we have allowed these sweeping changes to take place, simply assuming that the existing standards and tests represent our best educational interests. Instead, the mandates made upon teachers should be held up to the same level of scrutiny as the teachers themselves.

5

Value-Added Modeling Is the Best Tool to Measure Teacher Effectiveness

Steven Glazerman et al.

Steven Glazerman is a senior fellow at Mathematica Policy Research with expertise in methods for evaluating the impact of social programs and in teacher labor markets, including issues of teacher recruitment, professional development, alternative certification, performance measurement, and compensation.

A statistical method known as value-added modeling has enabled educational systems to estimate teachers' impacts on student learning by comparing student test scores at the beginning of the year to those at the end of the year, making statistical adjustments for factors outside the control of teachers. Although value-added evaluation is not perfect, it is the best system we currently have for evaluating teacher performance.

The vast majority of school districts presently employ teacher evaluation systems that result in all teachers receiving the same (top) rating. This is perhaps best exemplified by a recent [2010] report by the New Teacher Project focusing on thousands of teachers and administrators spanning twelve districts in four states. The report revealed that even though all the districts employed some formal evaluation process for teachers, all failed to differentiate meaningfully among levels of teaching effectiveness. In districts that used binary ratings

Steven Glazerman et al., "Evaluating Teachers: The Important Role of Value-Added," Brookings Institution, November 17, 2010. Copyright © 2010 by The Brookings Institution. All rights reserved. Reproduced by permission.

[a system with two options, satisfactory or unsatisfactory] more than 99 percent of teachers were rated satisfactory. In districts using a broader range of ratings, 94 percent received one of the top two ratings and less than 1 percent received an unsatisfactory rating. As Secretary of Education Arne Duncan put it, "Today in our country, 99 percent of our teachers are above average."

Teacher Evaluation at a Crossroads

There is an obvious need for teacher evaluation systems that include a spread of verifiable and comparable teacher evaluations that distinguish teacher effectiveness. We know from a large body of empirical research that teachers differ dramatically from one another in effectiveness. Evaluation systems could recognize these differences but they generally don't. As a consequence, the many low stakes and high stakes decisions that are made in the teacher labor market occur without the benefit of formalized recognition of how effective (or ineffective) teachers are in the classroom. Is there any doubt that teacher policy decisions would be better informed by teacher evaluation systems that meaningfully differentiate among teachers? . . .

Today in our country, 99 percent of our teachers are above average.

The latest generation of teacher evaluation systems seeks to incorporate information on the value-added by individual teachers to the achievement of their students. The teacher's contribution can be estimated in a variety of ways, but typically entails some variant of subtracting the achievement test score of a teacher's students at the beginning of the year from their score at the end of the year, and making statistical adjustments to account for differences in student learning that might result from student background or school-wide factors outside the teacher's control. These adjusted *gains* in student achievement are compared across teachers. Value-added scores can be expressed in a number of ways. One that is easy to grasp is a percentile score that indicates where a given teacher stands relative to other teachers. Thus a teacher who scored at the 75th percentile on value-added for mathematics achievement would have produced greater gains for her students than the gains produced by 75 percent of the other teachers being evaluated.

Critics of value-added methods have raised concerns about the statistical validity, reliability, and corruptibility of value-added measures. We believe the correct response to these concerns is to improve value-added measures continually and to use them wisely, not to discard or ignore the data. . . .

Value-Added Information vs. How to Use It

There is considerable debate about how teacher evaluations should be used to improve schools, and uncertainty about how to implement proposed reforms. For example, even those who favor linking pay to performance face numerous design decisions with uncertain consequences. How a pay for performance system is designed—salary incentives based on team performance vs. individual performance, having incentives managed from the state or district level vs. the building level, or having incentives structured as more rapid advancement through a system of ranks vs. annual bonuses—can result in very good or very ineffective policy.

Similar uncertainty surrounds other possible uses of value-added information. For example, tying tenure to value-added evaluation scores will have immediate effects on school performance that have been well modeled, but these models cannot predict indirect effects such as those that might result from changes in the profiles of people interested in entering the teaching profession. Such effects on the general equilibrium of the teacher labor market are largely the subject of hypothesis and speculation. Research on these and related topics is burgeoning, but right now much more is unknown than known.

However, uncertainties surrounding how best to design human resource policies that take advantage of meaningful teacher evaluation do not bear directly on the question of whether value-added information should be included as a component of teacher evaluation. There is considerable confusion between issues surrounding the inclusion of value-added scores in teacher evaluation systems and questions about how such information is used for human resource decisions. This is probably because the uses of teacher evaluation that have gained the most public attention or notoriety have been based *exclusively* on value-added. For example, in August 2010, the *Los Angeles Times* used several years of math and English test data to identify publicly the best and the worst third- to fifth-grade teachers in the Los Angeles Unified School District. The ensuing controversy focused as much on value-added evaluation as the newspaper's actions. But the question of whether these kinds of statistics should be published is separable from the question of whether such data should have a role in personnel decisions. It is routine for working professionals to receive consequential evaluations of their job performance, but that information is *not* typically broadcast to the public.

A Place for Value-Added

Much of the controversy surrounding teacher performance measures that incorporate value-added information is based on fears about how the measures will be used. After all, once administrators have ready access to a quantitative performance measure, they can use it for sensitive human resources decisions including teacher pay, promotion, or layoffs. They may or may not do this wisely or well, and it is reasonable for those who will be affected to express concerns.

We believe that whenever human resource actions are based on *evaluations* of teachers they will benefit from incorporating all the best available information, which includes value-added measures. Not only do teachers typically receive scant feedback on their past performance in raising test scores, the information they usually receive on the average test scores or proficiency of their students can be misleading or demoralizing. High test scores or a high proficiency rate may be more informative of who their students are than how they were taught. Low test scores might mask the incredible progress the teachers made. Teachers and their mentors and principals stand to gain vast new insight if they could see the teachers' performance placed in context of other teachers with students just like their own, drawn from a much larger population than a single school. This is the promise of value-added analysis. It is not a perfect system of measurement but it can complement observational measures, parent feedback, and personal reflections on teaching far better than any available alternative. It can be used to help guide resources to where they are needed most, to identify teachers' strengths and weaknesses, and to put a spotlight on the critical role of teachers in learning. . . .

Recent reports by nationally visible education researchers and thinkers have urged restraint in the use of teacher evaluations based on student test scores for high stakes decisions. The common thread in these reports is the concern that value-added scores reported at the level of individual teachers frequently misclassify teachers in ways that are unfair to teachers, e.g., identifying a teacher as ineffective who is in fact average.

There are three problems with these reports. First, they often set up an impossible test that is not the objective of any specific teacher evaluation system, such as using a single year of test score growth to produce a rank ordered list of teachers for a high stakes decision such as tenure. Any practical application of value-added measures should make use of confidence intervals in order to avoid false precision, and should include multiple years of value-added data in combination with other sources of information to increase reliability and validity. Second, they often ignore the fact that all decision-making systems have classification error. The goal is to minimize the most costly classification mistakes, not eliminate all of them. Third, they focus too much on one type of classification error, the type that negatively affects the interests of individual teachers. . . .

Value-added is superior to other existing methods of classifying teachers.

Much of the concern and cautions about the use of value-added have focused on the frequency of occurrence of false negatives, i.e., effective teachers who are identified as ineffective. But framing the problem in terms of false negatives places the focus almost entirely on the interests of the individual who is being evaluated rather than the students who are being served. It is easy to identify with the *good* teacher who wants to avoid dismissal for being incorrectly labeled a *bad* teacher. From that individual's perspective, no rate of misclassification is acceptable. However, an evaluation system that results in tenure and advancement for almost every teacher and thus has a very low rate of false negatives generates a high rate of false positives, i.e., teachers identified as effective who are not. These teachers drag down the performance of schools and do not serve students as well as more effective teachers. . . .

Ignoring Value-Added Data Does Not Help

We know a good deal about how other means of classification of teachers perform versus value-added. Rather than asking value-added to measure up to an arbitrary standard of perfection, it would be productive to ask how it performs compared to classification based on other forms of available information of teachers.

The "compared to what" question has been addressed by a good deal of research on the other teacher credentials and characteristics that are presently used to determine employment eligibility and compensation. Here the research is quite clear: if student test achievement is the outcome, value-added is superior to other existing methods of classifying teachers. Classification that relies on other measurable characteristics of teachers (e.g., scores on licensing tests, routes into teaching, nature of certification, National Board certification, teaching experience, quality of undergraduate institution, relevance of undergraduate coursework, extent and nature of professional development), considered singly or in aggregate, is not in the same league in terms of predicting future performance as evaluation based on value-added. . . .

Value-Added Has an Important Role to Play

We have a lot to learn about how to improve the reliability of value-added and other sources of information on teacher effectiveness, as well as how to build useful personnel policies around such information. However, too much of the debate about value-added assessment of teacher effectiveness has proceeded without consideration of the alternatives and by conflating objectionable personnel policies with value-added information itself. When teacher evaluation that incorporates value-added data is compared against an abstract ideal, it can easily be found wanting in that it provides only a fuzzy signal. But when it is compared to performance assessment in other fields or to evaluations of teachers based on other sources of information, it looks respectable and appears to provide the best signal we've got.

Teachers differ dramatically in their performance, with large consequences for students. Staffing policies that ignore this lose one of the strongest levers for lifting the performance of schools and students. That is why there is great interest in establishing teacher evaluation systems that meaningfully differentiate performance.

Teaching is a complex task and value-added captures only a portion of the impact of differences in teacher effectiveness. Thus high stakes decisions based on value-added measures of teacher performance will be imperfect. We do not advocate using value-added measures alone when making decisions about hiring, firing, tenure, compensation, placement, or developing teachers, but surely value-added information ought to be in the mix given the empirical evidence that it predicts more about what students will learn from the teachers to which they are assigned than any other source of information.

6

Value-Added Modeling Does Not Fully Measure Teacher Effectiveness

Eva L. Baker et al.

Eva L. Baker is a professor of education at UCLA and co-director of the National Center for Evaluation Standards and Student Testing.

Although value-added modeling, which makes adjustments to test scores based on certain student and school characteristics, has some value as a way of measuring educational progress, it should not be the only criterion used to judge teacher effectiveness. A variety of factors, such as attendance rates, out-of-school learning experiences, and class size, have an impact on student performance on standardized tests. Holding teachers solely accountable for student performance can discourage teachers from collaborating and also from working in schools with high-need children.

Every classroom should have a well-educated, professional teacher, and school systems should recruit, prepare, and retain teachers who are qualified to do the job. Yet in practice, American public schools generally do a poor job of systematically developing and evaluating teachers.

Many policy makers have recently come to believe that this failure can be remedied by calculating the improvement

Eva L. Baker et al., "Problems with the Use of Student Test Scores to Evaluate Teachers," *EPI Briefing Paper*, no. 278, August 29, 2010. Copyright © 2010 by Economic Policy Holder. All rights reserved. Reproduced by permission.

in students' scores on standardized tests in mathematics and reading, and then relying heavily on these calculations to evaluate, reward, and remove the teachers of these tested students.

Student Test Scores Are Only One Factor

While there are good reasons for concern about the current system of teacher evaluation, there are also good reasons to be concerned about claims that measuring teachers' effectiveness largely by student test scores will lead to improved student achievement. If new laws or policies specifically require that teachers be fired if their students' test scores do not rise by a certain amount, then more teachers might well be terminated than is now the case. But there is not strong evidence to indicate either that the departing teachers would actually be the weakest teachers, or that the departing teachers would be replaced by more effective ones. There is also little or no evidence for the claim that teachers will be more motivated to improve student learning if teachers are evaluated or monetarily rewarded for student test score gains.

A review of the technical evidence leads us to conclude that, although standardized test scores of students are one piece of information for school leaders to use to make judgments about teacher effectiveness, such scores should be only a part of an overall comprehensive evaluation. Some states are now considering plans that would give as much as 50% of the weight in teacher evaluation and compensation decisions to scores on existing tests of basic skills in math and reading. Based on the evidence, we consider this unwise. Any sound evaluation will necessarily involve a balancing of many factors that provide a more accurate view of what teachers in fact do in the classroom and how that contributes to student learning.

Evidence About the Use of Test Scores

Recent statistical advances have made it possible to look at student achievement gains after adjusting for some student and school characteristics. These approaches that measure growth using "value-added modeling" (VAM) are fairer comparisons of teachers than judgments based on their students' test scores at a single point in time or comparisons of student cohorts [a group of people with a statistic in common] that involve different students at two points in time. VAM methods have also contributed to stronger analyses of school progress, program influences, and the validity of evaluation methods than were previously possible.

Nonetheless, there is broad agreement among statisticians, psychometricians [those who administer and interpret psychological tests], and economists that student test scores alone are not sufficiently reliable and valid indicators of teacher effectiveness to be used in high-stakes personnel decisions, even when the most sophisticated statistical applications such as value-added modeling are employed.

For a variety of reasons, analyses of VAM results have led researchers to doubt whether the methodology can accurately identify more and less effective teachers. VAM estimates have proven to be unstable across statistical models, years, and classes that teachers teach. One study found that across five large urban districts, among teachers who were ranked in the top 20% of effectiveness in the first year, fewer than a third were in that top group the next year, and another third moved all the way down to the bottom 40%. Another found that teachers' effectiveness ratings in one year could only predict from 4% to 16% of the variation in such ratings in the following year. Thus, a teacher who appears to be very ineffective in one year might have a dramatically different result the following year. The same dramatic fluctuations were found for teachers ranked at the bottom in the first year of analysis. This runs counter to most peoples notions that the true quality of a teacher is likely to change very little over time and raises questions about whether what is measured is largely a "teacher effect" or the effect of a wide variety of other factors.

A study designed to test this question used VAM methods to assign effects to teachers after controlling for other factors, but applied the model backwards to see if credible results were obtained. Surprisingly, it found that students' fifth grade teachers were good predictors of their *fourth* grade test scores. Inasmuch as a student's later fifth grade teacher cannot possibly have influenced that student's fourth grade performance, this curious result can only mean that VAM results are based on factors other than teachers' actual effectiveness.

VAM's instability can result from differences in the characteristics of students assigned to particular teachers in a particular year, from small samples of students (made even less representative in schools serving disadvantaged students by high rates of student mobility), from other influences on student learning both inside and outside school, and from tests that are poorly lined up with the curriculum teachers are expected to cover, or that do not measure the full range of achievement of students in the class.

For these and other reasons, the research community has cautioned against the heavy reliance on test scores, even when sophisticated VAM methods are used, for high stakes decisions such as pay, evaluation, or tenure. For instance, the Board on Testing and Assessment of the National Research Council of the National Academy of Sciences stated, . . .

> VAM estimates of teacher effectiveness should not be used to make operational decisions because such estimates are far too unstable to be considered fair or reliable.

A review of VAM research from the Educational Testing Service's Policy Information Center concluded,

> VAM results should not serve as the sole or principal basis for making consequential decisions about teachers. There are many pitfalls to making causal attributions of teacher effectiveness on the basis of the kinds of data available from typical school districts. We still lack sufficient understanding

of how seriously the different technical problems threaten the validity of such interpretations.

And RAND Corporation researchers reported that,

> The estimates from VAM modeling of achievement will often be too imprecise to support some of the desired inferences ...

and that

> The research base is currently insufficient to support the use of VAM for high-stakes decisions about individual teachers or schools.

Factors Influencing Student Test Score Gains

A number of factors have been found to have strong influences on student learning gains, aside from the teachers to whom their scores would be attached. These include the influences of students' other teachers—both previous teachers and, in secondary schools, current teachers of other subjects—as well as tutors or instructional specialists, who have been found often to have very large influences on achievement gains. These factors also include school conditions—such as the quality of curriculum materials, specialist or tutoring supports, class size, and other factors that affect learning. Schools that have adopted pull-out, team teaching, or block scheduling practices will only inaccurately be able to isolate individual teacher "effects" for evaluation, pay, or disciplinary purposes.

Student test score gains are also strongly influenced by school attendance and a variety of out-of-school learning experiences at home, with peers, at museums and libraries, in summer programs, on-line, and in the community. Well-educated and supportive parents can help their children with homework and secure a wide variety of other advantages for them. Other children have parents who, for a variety of reasons, are unable to support their learning academically. Student test score gains are also influenced by family resources, student health, family mobility, and the influence of neighborhood peers and of classmates who may be relatively more advantaged or disadvantaged.

Teachers' value-added evaluations in low-income communities can be further distorted by the summer learning loss their students experience between the time they are tested in the spring and the time they return to school in the fall. Research shows that summer gains and losses are quite substantial. A research summary concludes that while students overall lose an average of about one month in reading achievement over the summer, lower-income students lose significantly more, and middle-income students may actually gain in reading proficiency over the summer, creating a widening achievement gap. Indeed, researchers have found that three-fourths of schools identified as being in the bottom 20% of all schools, based on the scores of students during the school year, would not be so identified if differences in learning outside of school were taken into account. Similar conclusions apply to the bottom 5% of all schools.

> *Individual teacher rewards based on comparative student test results can ... create disincentives for teacher collaboration.*

For these and other reasons, even when methods are used to adjust statistically for student demographic factors and school differences, teachers have been found to receive lower "effectiveness" scores when they teach new English learners, special education students, and low-income students than when they teach more affluent and educationally advantaged students. The nonrandom assignment of students to classrooms and schools—and the wide variation in students' experiences at home and at school—mean that teachers cannot be accurately judged against one another by their students' test scores, even when efforts are made to control for student characteristics in statistical models.

Recognizing the technical and practical limitations of what test scores can accurately reflect, we conclude that changes in test scores should be used only as a modest part of a broader set of evidence about teacher practice.

The Potential Consequences of Inappropriate Use

Besides concerns about statistical methodology, other practical and policy considerations weigh against heavy reliance on student test scores to evaluate teachers. Research shows that an excessive focus on basic math and reading scores can lead to narrowing and over-simplifying the curriculum to only the subjects and formats that are tested, reducing the attention to science, history, the arts, civics, and foreign language, as well as to writing, research, and more complex problem-solving tasks.

Tying teacher evaluation and sanctions to test score results can discourage teachers from wanting to work in schools with the neediest students, while the large, unpredictable variation in the results and their perceived unfairness can undermine teacher morale. Surveys have found that teacher attrition and demoralization have been associated with test-based accountability efforts, particularly in high-need schools.

Individual teacher rewards based on comparative student test results can also create disincentives for teacher collaboration. Better schools are collaborative institutions where teachers work across classroom and grade-level boundaries toward the common goal of educating all children to their maximum potential. A school will be more effective if its teachers are more knowledgeable about all students and can coordinate efforts to meet students' needs.

Some other approaches, with less reliance on test scores, have been found to improve teachers' practice while identifying differences in teachers' effectiveness. They use systematic observation protocols with well-developed, research-based criteria to examine teaching, including observations or videotapes of classroom practice, teacher interviews, and artifacts such as lesson plans, assignments, and samples of student work. Quite often, these approaches incorporate several ways of looking at student learning over time in relation to a teacher's instruction.

> *There is simply no shortcut to the identification and removal of ineffective teachers.*

Evaluation by competent supervisors and peers, employing such approaches, should form the foundation of teacher evaluation systems, with a supplemental role played by multiple measures of student learning gains that, where appropriate, could include test scores. Some districts have found ways to identify, improve, and as necessary, dismiss teachers using strategies like peer assistance and evaluation that offer intensive mentoring and review panels. These and other approaches should be the focus of experimentation by states and districts.

Adopting an invalid teacher evaluation system and tying it to rewards and sanctions is likely to lead to inaccurate personnel decisions and to demoralize teachers, causing talented teachers to avoid high-needs students and schools, or to leave the profession entirely, and discouraging potentially effective teachers from entering it. Legislatures should not mandate a test-based approach to teacher evaluation that is unproven and likely to harm not only teachers, but also the children they instruct. . . .

Alternatives Should Be Explored

Used with caution, value-added modeling can add useful information to comprehensive analyses of student progress and can help support stronger inferences about the influences of teachers, schools, and programs on student growth. . . .

There is simply no shortcut to the identification and removal of ineffective teachers. It must surely be done, but such actions will unlikely be successful if they are based on over-reliance on student test scores whose flaws can so easily provide the basis for successful challenges to any personnel action. Districts seeking to remove ineffective teachers must invest the time and resources in a comprehensive approach to evaluation that incorporates concrete steps for the improvement of teacher performance based on professional standards of instructional practice, and unambiguous evidence for dismissal, if improvements do not occur.

Some policy makers, acknowledging the inability fairly to identify effective or ineffective teachers by their students' test scores, have suggested that low test scores (or value-added estimates) should be a "trigger" that invites further investigation. Although this approach seems to allow for multiple means of evaluation, in reality 100% of the weight in the trigger is test scores. Thus, all the incentives to distort instruction will be preserved to avoid identification by the trigger, and other means of evaluation will enter the system only after it is too late to avoid these distortions.

While those who evaluate teachers could take student test scores over time into account, they should be fully aware of their limitations, and such scores should be only one element among many considered in teacher profiles. Some states are now considering plans that would give as much as 50% of the weight in teacher evaluation and compensation decisions to scores on existing poor-quality tests of basic skills in math and reading. Based on the evidence we have reviewed above, we consider this unwise. If the quality, coverage, and design of standardized tests were to improve, some concerns would be addressed, but the serious problems of attribution and non-random assignment of students, as well as the practical problems described above, would still argue for serious limits on the use of test scores for teacher evaluation.

Although some advocates argue that admittedly flawed value-added measures are preferred to existing cumbersome measures for identifying, remediating, or dismissing ineffective teachers, this argument creates a false dichotomy. It implies there are only two options for evaluating teachers—the ineffectual current system or the deeply flawed test-based system.

Yet there are many alternatives that should be the subject of experiments. The Department of Education should actively encourage states to experiment with a range of approaches that differ in the ways in which they evaluate teacher practice and examine teachers' contributions to student learning. These experiments should all be fully evaluated.

There is no perfect way to evaluate teachers. However, progress has been made over the last two decades in developing standards-based evaluations of teaching practice, and research has found that the use of such evaluations by some districts has not only provided more useful evidence about teaching practice, but has also been associated with student achievement gains and has helped teachers improve their practice and effectiveness. Structured performance assessments of teachers like those offered by the National Board for Professional Teaching Standards and the beginning teacher assessment systems in Connecticut and California have also been found to predict teacher's effectiveness on value-added measures and to support teacher learning.

These systems for observing teachers' classroom practice are based on professional teaching standards grounded in research on teaching and learning. They use systematic observation protocols with well-developed, research-based criteria to examine teaching, including observations or videotapes of classroom practice, teacher interviews, and artifacts such as lesson plans, assignments, and samples of student work. Quite often, these approaches incorporate several ways of looking at student learning over time in relation to the teacher's instruction.

Evaluation by competent supervisors and peers, employing such approaches, should form the foundation of teacher evaluation systems, with a supplemental role played by multiple measures of student learning gains that, where appropriate, should include test scores. Given the importance of teachers' collective efforts to improve overall student achievement in a school, an additional component of documenting practice and outcomes should focus on the effectiveness of teacher participation in teams and the contributions they make to school-wide improvement, through work in curriculum development, sharing practices and materials, peer coaching and reciprocal observation, and collegial work with students.

In some districts, peer assistance and review programs—using standards-based evaluations that incorporate evidence of student learning, supported by expert teachers who can offer intensive assistance, and panels of administrators and teachers that oversee personnel decisions—have been successful in coaching teachers, identifying teachers for intervention, providing them assistance, and efficiently counseling out those who do not improve. In others, comprehensive systems have been developed for examining teacher performance in concert with evidence about outcomes for purposes of personnel decision making and compensation.

Given the range of measures currently available for teacher evaluation, and the need for research about their effective implementation and consequences, legislatures should avoid imposing mandated solutions to the complex problem of identifying more and less effective teachers. School districts should be given freedom to experiment, and professional organizations should assume greater responsibility for developing standards of evaluation that districts can use. Such work, which must be performed by professional experts, should not be preempted by political institutions acting without evidence. The rule followed by any reformer of public schools should be: "First, do no harm."

As is the case in every profession that requires complex practice and judgments, precision and perfection in the evaluation of teachers will never be possible. Evaluators may find it useful to take student test score information into account in their evaluations of teachers, provided such information is embedded in a more comprehensive approach. What is now necessary is a comprehensive system that gives teachers the guidance and feedback, supportive leadership, and working conditions to improve their performance, and that permits schools to remove persistently ineffective teachers without distorting the entire instructional program by imposing a flawed system of standardized quantification of teacher quality.

7

The Pressure to Meet Targets Has Caused Teachers to Cheat

Teacher World

Teacher World *is a website offering articles and resource material about teacher education.*

In July 2011, the Georgia Bureau of Investigation released a report on the Atlanta Public Schools charging a widespread cheating conspiracy over a ten-year period by 178 teachers, principals, and administrators to fix answers on the statewide Criterion-Referenced Competency Test. The report concluded that unreasonable targets combined with a superintendent who would not accept failure created an atmosphere in which teachers and principals felt they had to cheat to keep their jobs. Atlanta is not the only school system to resort to cheating. The targets mandated by No Child Left Behind are unreasonable and are causing irreparable damage to the education system.

[I]t is clear that things began to change [in the Atlanta Public Schools (APS)] in 1999, when Dr. Beverly Hall became the superintendent of APS. How could one person be blamed for jump-starting the madness? Well, Hall was all about data and reaching targets. And she set up a "target" program which held principals and teachers responsible for their students' achievement. According to the [GBI (Georgia Bureau of Investigation)] report, "These targets were used to quantify expectations so that academic progress was measurable, based primarily on the prior year's CRCT [Criterion-Referenced Competency Test] results."

"GBI Reveals Why Cheating Occurred in Atlanta Public Schools," Teacher World, July 10, 2011, www.teacher-world.com. Copyright © 2011 by All-Star Directories. All rights reserved. Reproduced by permission.

Pressure to Meet Targets Caused Cheating

According to the report, "The unreasonable pressure to meet annual 'targets' was the primary motivation for teachers and administration to cheat on the CRCT in 2009 and previous years. Virtually every teacher who confessed to cheating spoke of the inordinate stress the district placed on meeting targets and the dire consequences for failure. Dr. Hall articulated it as: 'No exceptions. No excuses.' If principals did not meet targets within three years, she declared, they will be replaced and 'I will find someone who will meet targets.' Dr. Hall replaced 90% of the principals during her tenure. Principals told teachers that failure to improve CRCT scores would result in negative evaluations or job termination. The unambiguous message was to meet targets by any means necessary."

The unambiguous message was to meet targets by any means necessary.

Under the target program used in APS, schools were expected to move students' test scores in two ways: from the bottom to the middle, and from the middle to the top, which means focusing on both the lower and higher performing students.

Targets were set each year by the administration working with outside consultants, which were then approved by the Board of Education. These targets were set for the district, for each school, and for each grade based on percentages of expected improvement, which were naturally higher for low-performing schools.

The Targets Were Unreasonable

Keep in mind that as schools met their targets, those targets would increase each year. And the new targets weren't based upon the new students coming into a grade level, but the scores achieved by the previous year's students.

If you are a teacher, you know that each year's students have their own strengths and weaknesses and have different levels of motivation. This target program makes no accommodations for those differences; instead the expectation is that each year there is a certain percent increase in student progress no matter what each group's strengths or weaknesses might be.

Teachers and administrators at APS told investigators that "this element of targets, combined with the fact that the targets increase every year, makes them unreasonable. For instance, if last year's fourth graders were mostly high-performing students, but the fourth grade class this year contains more low performers, the fourth grade targets are still set based on last year's high performing students' scores." As teachers reported to investigators, it was like comparing apples to oranges.

The cheating, once started, took on a life of its own.

As targets continued to increase each year, teachers reported that it was harder to attain the required results, and many resorted to cheating rather than risk disciplinary action or termination. It became that proverbial snowball effect; each year it required more cheating in order to go beyond the level of cheating the previous year in order to meet the new unreasonable target. And "the gap between where the students were academically and the targets they were trying to reach grew larger." The cheating, once started, took on a life of its own.

Fear Was a Greater Motivator than Greed

While some of those who cheated were motivated by bonuses (schools that met 70% of their targeted goals received bonuses for all of their employees ranging anywhere from $50 to $2000 per employee) most of them seemed to be more motivated by their fear of recrimination if they were unsuccessful in meeting their targets. (A little sidebar from the GBI report that you might find interesting: Dr. Hall received tens of thousands of dollars based on her district's doctored CRCT results.)

And to sweeten the pot a little more to motivate staffs, the district held a celebration annually at the Georgia Dome to honor and recognize those schools which had made their targets. At the Convocation, attendance from all schools was mandatory, and those who were being recognized for a job well-done got to "make the floor," that is, they got to sit in a prominent place on the floor of the Dome, while those who did not reach their targets were forced to sit in the uppermost sections.

The report noted that for many it became very important to "make the floor," especially for principals. For these individuals, the means by which this was accomplished became unimportant; the recognition, even if it was a fabricated sham, was so much better than the humiliation of sitting in the nose-bleed section.

Those schools who failed to meet their targets were usually placed on PDP's, professional development plans. The original purpose of a professional development plan was to provide a tool for helping a staff to improve areas of weakness, in other words, to provide a low-performing school some strategies and professional development which would enable it to turn around and achieve success.

However, under Dr. Hall's leadership, a PDP brought negative performance evaluations, threats of termination, and for some, outright termination. She made it clear that if these low-performing schools did not reach their targets in three years, she would replace the principal with someone who would find a way to meet those targets. . . .

It comes as no surprise that those principals who feared that they would lose their jobs reciprocated in kind, putting that same negative pressure with its unreasonable expectations and demands on their teachers. And the pattern of threats and humiliation and termination became acceptable at all levels of this school district, which operated more like the mafia than a school system.

No Child Left Behind Has Damaged Education

It is hard to say how any of us, placed in this hostile and vicious work environment would have reacted. I would like to think that the majority of us would have stood our ground and refused to be a part of this criminal behavior against children. But in this educational environment in which test scores have become more important than the children we teach, should we be so surprised when it creates a monster?

What is wrong with education? The scandal in Atlanta makes it very clear, and they are not the only school district to resort to cheating to improve test scores. No Child Left Behind [NCLB] has done more damage to our public schools than any doctrine or educational reform I have ever seen as a veteran teacher. If Congress doesn't wake up and heed [US Secretary of Education] Arne Duncan's warnings to rewrite NCLB legislation, than what we have seen here over the past week is just the tip of the iceberg.

If nothing else, APS has proven what can happen when you are sailing in troubled waters. The 2014 iceberg is looming, and unless Congress reroutes this ship, we will all be witnesses to the tragic sinking of our public education system.

8

Cheating on Test Scores Does Not Invalidate the Need for Testing

Saba Bireda

Saba Bireda, formerly an education policy analyst at the Center for American Progress, is deputy director of the Poverty & Race Research Action Council.

Many educators have concluded that the emphasis placed on testing and accountability by the No Child Left Behind legislation created an atmosphere that caused the cheating scandal in the Atlanta Public Schools. The answer is not to conclude that testing is bad, but to create a better methodology of testing and measures for holding teachers accountable for results.

The allegations of massive fraud in public school test scores show that educators are focused more on avoiding failure than on teaching children better, says this education advocate.

We teach children that "cheaters never win." Unfortunately for the students of the Atlanta Public Schools [APS], it's a lesson that the adults in charge have apparently not yet learned. Last week a state investigation found evidence that more than 150 APS staff members directly participated in or knew of schemes to change student answer sheets to reflect correct answers.

The news is devastating for a school system widely regarded as defying the odds and increasing achievement among

Saba Bireda, "Your Take: Lessons from the Atlanta Cheating Scandal," *The Root*, July 12, 2011. Copyright © 2011 by The Root. All rights reserved. Reproduced by permission.

its low-income, mostly African-American students. The gains reported by the Atlanta public school system garnered millions of dollars in private funds and accolades for Superintendent Beverly Hall. APS' success, which Hall attributed to standards-based instruction and strong professional development for teachers, was also a boon to supporters of traditional public school systems, who believe that reform is possible without overreliance on charter schools and with dramatic changes in teaching policy.

The Atlanta incident has led many education spectators to conclude that an overemphasis on standardized testing and the federal accountability system under No Child Left Behind [NCLB] created an atmosphere in which teachers had to cheat. The state report 'certainly provides ample fodder for this view. It describes dysfunction across the system, with several teachers told either to falsify answers or to face termination.

We should resist efforts to halt testing altogether or to return to a time when school failure could go largely unaddressed.

Atlanta's troubles demonstrate some of the worst outcomes of a test-based accountability system. Rather than miss performance targets set by a seemingly out-of-touch administration, some educators chose to take matters into their own hands. They often succeeded in avoiding the fate of many urban schools: being labeled as "failing" under NCLB's accountability structure. In the process, the desire to avoid negative repercussions seemed to eclipse concerns about student progress. Among the most disheartening details from the report are quotes from a teacher who thought her students were just too "dumb" to do well on the test.

Abandoning Testing Is Not the Solution

As alarming as this scandal is, we should resist efforts to halt testing altogether or to return to a time when school failure could go largely unaddressed. We must create a better system of tests and accountability, not only to avoid continued disillusionment with reform efforts but also to refocus the work of schools and teachers on teaching and learning.

It's not a surprise that reports of cheating and overstressed teachers have produced a negative attitude toward the use of tests. But standardized tests, when reflective of standards and curriculum, can be a useful tool for teachers. The data from tests can inform teachers of the knowledge their students have gained and what they still need to learn.

Tests are particularly useful in helping teachers understand where their students fall in comparison with other students. Without such tests, many states and school systems would be able to conceal wide disparities in the quality of education provided to students of different races and socioeconomic backgrounds.

The Existing Accountability System Does Not Work

More often than not, schools in both low- and high-income communities where students are actually learning are not where teachers are so worried about test scores that they feel forced to cheat. Instead, successful schools and districts provide their students with high-quality instruction, engaging curriculums and supports that deliver sustained student achievement. In my own experience as a teacher, I found that teaching the plays of August Wilson, turning vocabulary quizzes into *Jeopardy* games and spending extra time with struggling readers yielded much more success on those tests than drills on synonyms and antonyms did.

Obviously, the administrators and teachers at many schools don't feel that emphasizing these factors will ensure success in the current accountability system. They may be right. NCLB pushed states to set goals for students to be "proficient" in reading and math by 2014. But the law's response to schools that fail to meet these goals didn't cause schools to double down on efforts to recruit great teachers or figure out new ways to teach math. Instead, schools became more focused on avoiding the law's gradually increasing sanctions.

Schools (and teachers) that continually fail students have to change.

Almost everyone in education—from parents to the president—agrees that this accountability system doesn't work. A new approach should encourage the kind of effective teaching and meaningful learning that leads students to success beyond any single year of test data. At the same time, schools (and teachers) that continually fail students have to change.

The Need for School Culture Change

Expanding the criteria for rating schools may reduce the myopic focus on standardized test results. Such an assessment should cover factors that increase student achievement, including instruction, funding and support for students.

Standardized tests also have a place in the evaluation of schools. When students repeatedly do poorly on tests that accurately measure their knowledge, we should be examining the reasons. The challenge for policymakers is to craft the appropriate responses to any sign of school failure, whether it's a lack of competent school leadership or insufficient lab tools for students to learn science.

There is no foolproof way to guard against cheating in a system where adults are ultimately responsible for student learning. But when education policy focuses on creating and supporting academic environments in which learning is the goal, school cultures will likely change from test-focused to student-focused. That's a lesson worth teaching our children.

9

No Child Left Behind Testing Has Produced Benefits

Greg Forster

Greg Forster is a senior fellow at the Foundation for Educational Choice.

Although the stated goal of No Child Left Behind (NCLB)—to have 100 percent of all students pass the proficiency test by 2014—is unachievable and absurd, NCLB has brought considerable benefits. Standardized tests and standardized reporting on the results have enabled educators to more accurately measure what does and does not work in education.

The deadline is looming for reauthorization of No Child Left Behind (NCLB), the law that says states getting federal education subsidies must give standardized tests and make regular progress toward 100% student proficiency in 2014. Naturally, there's a fierce debate going on about whether the law should be extended. [NLCB was not reauthorized in 2008 and has not been reauthorized as of August 2011.]

The official justification—that NCLB would make 100% of students proficient—doesn't pass the laugh test. But the arguments that it harms education, though they seem much more plausible, are also misplaced. And a federal mandate for testing produces important benefits that are well worth the costs.

We were never going to get 100% of kids to pass any kind of test, but that's the line that's been used to sell NCLB. States

Greg Forster, "Critics Miss Benefits of 'No Child Left Behind,'" pajamasmedia.com, May 16, 2008. Copyright © 2008 by PJ Media. All rights reserved. Reproduced by permission.

must set goals for the percentage of students who will pass the test in each year, with the goals increasing up to 100% in 2014. Any school with a demographic subgroup of students that remains below the targeted pass rate for multiple years is subject to sanctions.

If you have any experience with politics, you've already guessed what the states' multi-year improvement plans look like. They anticipate slow gains over the first eight to ten years, then a huge explosion in student proficiency in the last few years.

This is, of course, an old political game. You do what you really want to do right away, and in order to sell it to the public, you make impossible promises whose fulfillment is postponed until later.

If the official case for NCLB is bogus, it doesn't follow that NCLB has been a bad thing.

Nonetheless, I've been amazed at how the NCLB coalition has stuck rigidly to the 100% proficiency message. I had expected that by now, they would be preparing the ground for the inevitable clawback. But no—in Washington it's still all systems go for 100% proficiency in 2014, powered by the magical explosion of learning scheduled to occur starting in about 2011.

The Arguments Against NCLB Do Not Hold Up

But if the official case for NCLB is bogus, it doesn't follow that NCLB has been a bad thing. The arguments that it harms education, while they aren't quite as insulting to the intelligence, don't stand up to scrutiny.

People complain that the school sanctions are severe. But only a few schools are even hypothetically subject to serious sanctions, and those that are can take advantage of huge loopholes.

People complain that implementing the law's testing requirement is expensive. But it isn't. And anyway, NCLB showers schools with huge new subsidies—that's the only reason it passed.

People complain that the mandate produces teaching to the test. But that's another way of saying it makes sure schools teach what they're supposed to. Research shows that accountability tests measure real knowledge, not just test-taking skills.

People complain that testing basic skills cuts into other subjects. There's not much evidence that's actually happening, but even if it is, it would only be because schools need more time to teach basic skills right. And if kids can't read, how are they going to learn other subjects?

People complain that NCLB violates federalism. But states can get out of NCLB by simply refusing federal subsidies.

NCLB's more cogent critics complain that it creates incentives to dumb down the proficiency standard until everyone is "proficient." But that happens anyway. State standards have always been vulnerable to downward pressure; NCLB changes little in this regard. There's no evidence that dumbing down is occurring more frequently now than it always has.

The amount of empirical research done on education has been growing at a breathtaking rate.

When you set aside all the implausible multi-year plans, toothless sanctions, easily evaded school choice requirements, and other window dressing, NCLB boils down to one simple commercial transaction: the system got a big cash payoff, in exchange for which it agreed to give standardized tests and release up-to-date information on how students are performing.

The Growth in Actionable Research Is the Real Boon

Before NCLB, many states didn't give standardized tests at all, or didn't release the results in a timely and publicly useable format. Now they all do. And all 50 states now participate in the Nation's Report Card, a single national test of a representative sample of students, which allows researchers to conduct cross-state comparisons.

This transparency represents an incredible boon. The amount of empirical research done on education has been growing at a breathtaking rate. Before NCLB, education was a fringe element at best in economics, political science, and other social science disciplines. Now it's everywhere. A lot of that research is due to the data made available by NCLB.

Our knowledge of what works and what doesn't in education, and how best to measure it, is finally starting to grow after a century of dead ends and wrong turns. For example, it's now common knowledge in the education field that what counts isn't achievement levels, but year-to-year growth in achievement. How many people grasped that ten years ago?

This explosive increase in accurate information can only be good for the public—and for the cause of real reform, since defenders of the status quo rely primarily on myths and innuendo.

Sure, some states may tamper with the definition of "proficient." But the raw scale scores are publicly available, and independent researchers can, and do, use these scores to perform legitimate analyses to inform the public of how students are doing. . . .

What the issue really boils down to is whether we're going to know anything about education outcomes or not. Regardless of whether NCLB is reauthorized or not, some mandate for standardized testing as the price of getting federal subsidies is indispensable. If the feds are going to subsidize educa-

tion—and it seems that no force on earth can stop them—
they might as well demand transparency in return.

10

SAT Scores Help Colleges Make Better Decisions

Gaston Caperton

Gaston Caperton, former governor of West Virginia, is president of the College Board, the organization that owns and develops the SAT tests.

Research shows that the SAT test is an objective measure of college readiness and provides college admissions officers with a reliable tool to compare students. Research also has shown that the SAT test does not discriminate against any ethnic or racial group. Colleges that move to an SAT-optional policy often act to enhance their status and not in the best interests of their students.

Decision-making has been greatly aided in this age of technology by the availability of accurate data. The wise use of data was slow to be adopted in the field of education, but today it has become critical to the decision-making process. Secretary of Education Arne Duncan often talks about how the proper use of critical data sets can measure, monitor, and improve student performance. The "test-optional" policies that a few colleges now use in their admissions process are completely contrary to a national movement toward the use of more rather than fewer data in the decision-making process.

The SAT is the most widely used and most heavily researched college admissions test in the country. In combination with other data, such as a student's grade-point average

Gaston Caperton, "SATs Help Colleges Make Smarter Admissions Calls," *U.S. News & World Report*, September 4, 2009. Copyright © 2009 by U.S. News & World Report. All rights reserved. Reproduced by permission.

[GPA], college application essays, and letters of recommendation, the SAT has proven to be a valid, fair, and reliable data tool for college admissions. All of the available research supports this point. The great majority of our nation's colleges and universities accept the SAT as an integral part of the admissions process, and most that require the submission of the SAT do so because they know they can make better admissions decisions if they have as many data as possible about every student applicant.

The SAT has proven to be a valid, fair, and reliable data tool for college admissions.

The college admissions process is like most other activities in our increasingly complex society: The more data and information we have available, the better decisions we can make. Nearly all college admissions officers in the country share this perspective.

The SAT Is the Only Objective Measure

The SAT offers a standardized, level playing field in the admissions process, where grade inflation has made it difficult to weigh the real value of the GPA of a student from one school against that of a student from another. In 1987, 27 percent of SAT takers reported high school GPAs of A plus, A, or A minus; by 2007, this figure had grown to 43 percent.

That's one reason most college admissions officers tell us they rely on the SAT to be an objective measure of college readiness. It's often the only such measure at their disposal.

Test-optional colleges know that students who do well on the SAT will most likely submit their scores, while those who do poorly probably will not. The result is a higher average SAT score for their institution. Test-optional colleges also know that they will see an increase in their application pool, and if they still admit the same number of students as in the past, their percentage of admits will make them look more competitive in the ranking process.

While most test-optional institutions aren't necessarily trying to "game" the system in these ways, some experts argue that a few institutions have implemented a test-optional policy simply because it means greater national status for their college—not necessarily because it's in the best interest of students.

The SAT Is Not Biased Against Minorities

Some argue that the SAT is unfair to minority students, but the research clearly shows that the SAT is not biased against any ethnic or racial group. The College Board takes its mission very seriously: to connect students to college success, with a commitment to excellence and equity. The goal of the college admissions process is to help every student find a college that best matches his or her interests and needs. The more data that colleges have in helping make admissions decisions, the better they serve students and their families.

As the issue of standardized test use attests, college admissions is a difficult and complex process. Despite the challenges, colleges nationwide excel at helping students of all backgrounds ultimately achieve their dreams of a college degree, and it is a privilege to be a part of this critically important work.

11

Colleges Do Not Need SAT Scores to Be Selective in Admissions

Ann B. McDermott

Ann B. McDermott is director of admissions at the College of the Holy Cross in Worcester, MA.

Making SAT scores an optional part of the admissions process has worked extremely well for the College of the Holy Cross. After three years of an SAT-optional policy, Holy Cross has become more geographically and ethnically diverse as well as more selective in admissions, and the quality of applicants has improved. Students are the beneficiaries of this change in policy because they are rewarded for good choices and habits throughout their high school career, and not judged on the basis of a single test.

SAT scores still wield a mighty force in our culture and in the psyches of teenagers, even though 760 American colleges and universities, including my own, have made standardized testing an optional part of the admissions process. After admitting three classes of students under a testing-optional policy adopted in April 2005, I was startled this spring when I found it difficult to convince my own daughter, who was disappointed in her SAT scores, that her future is not dictated by the results of a test. She nodded when I, as a college-admissions officer, promised her that there are other, more-accurate measures of ability and success, and that a test score

Ann B. McDermott, "Surviving without the SAT," *The Chronicle of Higher Education*, October 10, 2008, vol, 55, no. 7. Copyright © 2008. All rights reserved. Reproduced by permission of author.

can never convey what she has experienced, learned, and accomplished. But I could see that all she was thinking about was that number.

I was able to assure my daughter without reservation, as an increasing number of institutions consider eliminating their testing requirements. While I admit it's a scary prospect—as is any major policy change—the benefits far outweigh the challenges and risks for all parties involved.

Becoming SAT-Optional Made Holy Cross More Diverse

For any college contemplating the change to test-optional, the report just issued by a commission convened by the National Association for College Admission Counseling is required reading. The commission spent a year examining the impact of standardized testing on the admissions process, and its recommendations provide further weight to test-optional policies. The commission advises colleges to scrutinize how they use test scores and urges them to place more emphasis on students' high-school curricula and achievements. Our experience at the College of the Holy Cross reaffirms those conclusions.

Three years ago, after the new writing portion of the SAT was unveiled, my college announced that it would make SAT and ACT scores an optional part of prospective students' applications. It was a carefully considered decision, made after several years of discussion and debate over the role that test scores played in our admissions process. Because Holy Cross had long placed more weight on a student's academic record, high-school courses, and qualitative evaluations than on standardized-test scores, the move was more a public announcement of an existing process than a major shift in how we made our admissions decisions.

Like other institutions making similar announcements—Wake Forest University and Smith College, most recently—

Holy Cross received national media attention. Like them, we were applauded by many guidance counselors, teachers, and parents. And we were roundly criticized by others.

Three years later, I can say that becoming SAT-optional has brought Holy Cross overwhelmingly positive results. The students admitted under the new policy are more geographically and ethnically diverse than previous classes were. Since 2006 the percentage of first-year students admitted from outside New England went from 46 percent to 50 percent; and the proportion of African-American, Latin American, Asian-American, and Native American students went from 17 percent to 21 percent. The three classes since 2006 are also statistically stronger, with more students taking the most-rigorous course loads available at their high schools. Reports from the faculty are positive, describing this group of students as engaged, focused, and truly committed to maximizing their Holy Cross experience. . . .

Becoming SAT-optional has brought Holy Cross overwhelmingly positive results.

Tests Can Distract Students

We knew from experience that great testers who didn't do well in high school were not the students who would thrive at Holy Cross, with its small class sizes, close student-faculty interaction, and rigorous liberal-arts program. Classroom work, writing, and intellectual exploration are more important indicators of success for us. We wanted to send the message that those are the things high school students should be spending time and energy on—not prepping for a test. In the process, we hoped to eliminate some of the stress that families and students experience in relation to testing.

We also empower prospective students by letting them know that they are active participants in the admissions process. We're not making a decision based on a single test score that can be skewed by factors—like socioeconomic status, parents' educational experiences, and access to test-preparation programs—that are beyond a student's control. Instead we evaluate students based on the four-year story they tell us through their transcripts, essays, and interviews. Their high-school career is concrete and real; they are the authors of their own narratives. By minimizing the distraction that testing brings to the high-school story, we get at the heart of what we know makes a great Holy Cross student—a willingness to work hard and an eagerness to learn. . . .

Holy Cross Became More Selective

The most immediate and unfounded response was that Holy Cross was lowering its standards. Some critics perceived that dropping the SATs from our process would somehow make us less competitive. . . .

In reality, Holy Cross became more selective. Our announcement did away with the notion that a stellar test score would secure admission. We sent a clear message that hard work over four years of high school was a better indicator of whether a student was right for Holy Cross. The year we went test-optional, our applications jumped 41 percent, and they have continued to increase. (To be honest, such a big one-year hike is probably due to several factors, not solely our testing policy.) This year the college had more applicants than ever before, 7,226. We accepted just over 30 percent to create the 720-member first-year class. The quality of our applicants has improved over the past three years as well. Students are in the top 7 percent of their high-school classes, compared with the previous figure of 10 percent. . . .

Results in High School Really Matter

There is, indeed, life after the SAT. Whether or not an institution opts for a test-optional policy, it is vital that young people understand that a test score does not define them. Colleges have a responsibility to help students see the value in their accomplishments and the opportunities that await.

It is vital that young people understand that a test score does not define them.

High-school students need to hear that they have control over their academic future, that the courses they choose and the direction they take in high school truly matter. Those of us in higher education should give them back such control and demystify what can be a bewildering process. Taking the focus off a number and broadening our discussions to include high-school course selection and classroom performance benefit both prospective students and colleges. Further, by eliminating arbitrary SAT-score cutoffs from admissions and scholarship opportunities, and steering away from discussions about the selectivity of a college based on a range of SAT scores, all of us—parents, teachers, and guidance and admissions counselors—can better serve our young people as they consider their next important chapter.

Even though my daughter had heard me talking at the dinner table for more than three years about the benefits for Holy Cross of moving to a test-optional policy, the power of a number momentarily took the wind out of her sails. Today I'm glad that she is excited about entering her senior year and eagerly anticipating what comes next. Minimizing the emphasis we place on the SAT can only mean maximizing our students' potential for success and happiness.

12

The SAT Test May Discriminate Against African Americans

Jay Mathews

Jay Mathews is an education columnist for The Washington Post.

New research confirms a claim made back in 2003 that the SAT discriminates against African Americans. The research shows that while white students on average performed better on easier questions in the verbal portion of the SAT, African-American students on average performed better than did whites on more difficult questions. Researchers believe this is because easier questions use more common words. Common words can be misinterpreted by African Americans because these words often have more meanings and different meanings in white than in minority neighborhoods.

Roy Freedle is 76 now, with a research psychologist's innate patience. He knows that decades often pass before valid ideas take root. When the notion is as radical as his, that the SAT is racially biased, an even longer wait might be expected. But after 23 years the research he has done on the surprising reaction of black students to hard words versus easy words seems to be gaining new respectability.

Jay Mathews, "New Evidence That SAT Hurts Blacks," *The Washington Post*, June 17, 2010. Copyright © 2010 by The Washington Post. All rights reserved. Reproduced by permission.

The SAT Is Biased

Seven years ago, after being discouraged from investigating findings while working for the Educational Testing Service [ETS], Freedle published a paper in the *Harvard Educational Review* that won significant attention.

He was retired from ETS by then. As he expected, his former supervisors dismissed his conclusions. Researchers working for the College Board, which owns the SAT, said the test was not biased. But the then president of the University of California system, a cognitive psychologist named Richard C. Atkinson, was intrigued. He asked the director of research in his office to replicate Freedle's study.

Now, in the latest issue of the Harvard Educational Review [June 2010], the two scholars who took on that project have published a paper saying Freedle was right about a flaw in the SAT, even in its current form. They say "the SAT, a high-stakes test with significant consequences for the educational opportunities available to young people in the United States, favors one ethnic group over another."

The SAT . . . favors one ethnic group over another.

"The confirmation of unfair test results throws into question the validity of the test and, consequently, all decisions based on its results," said Maria Veronica Santelices, now at the Pontificia Universidad Catolica de Chile in Santiago, and Mark Wilson of UC [University of California] Berkeley. "All admissions decisions based exclusively or predominantly on SAT performance—and therefore access to higher education institutions and subsequent job placement and professional success—appear to be biased against the African American minority group and could be exposed to legal challenge."

Researchers at the College Board and ETS don't like this new paper anymore than they liked Freedle's in 2003. Laurence Bunin, the College Board vice president in charge of the

SAT, said the Santelices-Wilson study is "fundamentally flawed." He pointed out that it had not yet been peer reviewed. He said the scholars' conclusions were "wrong and irresponsible and a disservice to students, parents and colleges," and were based on "a very small, limited and unrepresentative sample."

College Board spokeswoman Kathleen Steinberg said the Harvard Educational Review declined the College Board's offer of a response to the paper, but plans to publish a criticism of the paper by ETS researcher Neil Dorans, as well as a response by Freedle himself.

Word Complexity Is a Key Variable

They are discussing a complex topic, full of psychometric terms and concepts I am not competent to judge. Back in 2003, when I wrote a long article for the *Atlantic Monthly* on Freedle's work, I relied heavily on him and other experts to explain what they were talking about. Much of it had to do with a method of test analysis called differential item functioning, or DIF (rhymes with cliff). Psychometricians [those who design and analyze psychological studies] like Freedle and his colleagues at ETS, which was then managing the SAT, looked at how different ethnicities that were matched at different scoring levels (those who had scored 360 on the SAT verbal test, then those who had scored 380, and so on) did on each item.

At each level of ability, but particularly in the lower-scoring groups, white students on average did better than blacks on the easier items, whereas blacks on average did better than whites on the harder ones. (Whites, however, as a group did better overall.)

This was unexpected. The deeper Freedle got into it, the more uncomfortable his supervisors seemed to be with his work. He had to revise one paper more than 11 times before they allowed him to publish it.

Hard questions, those that produced more wrong answers, tended to have longer, less common words. Easy questions tended to have shorter, more common words. Freedle thought this was key to the relative success African American students had with the harder ones. Simpler words tended to have more meanings, and in some cases different meanings in white middle class neighborhoods than they had in underprivileged minority neighborhoods, he concluded. This, he said, could help explain why African American students did worse on questions with common words than on questions that depended on harder, but less ambiguous words they studied at school.

African American students did worse on questions with common words than on questions that depended on harder, but less ambiguous words.

Revised Calculation Proposed

On average, he said, black students were performing only slightly above matched-ability whites on hard questions. But averages did not submit applications to colleges. Individual students did. Some of those individuals, he discovered, would have gotten a boost of a hundred points or more on the SAT if the score was weighted toward the hard items. He proposed that the College Board offer a supplement to SAT scores, called the Revised-SAT, or R-SAT, which would be calculated based only on the hard items. This, he said, would "greatly increase the number of high-scoring minority individuals."

In their paper, Santelices and Wilson rule out Freedle's suggestion that the bias he found in the test might affect all kinds of multiple-choice questions, or minorities other than blacks. But they did find it in sentence completion and reading comprehension sections of the SAT.

Saul Geiser was the director of research in Atkinson's office originally given the assignment to look into Freedle's theory. Eventually he arranged for Santelices, then a doctoral candidate at UC Berkeley, to do the research as her PhD thesis, working with Wilson, a UC Berkeley psychometrician who had also been asked to look at Freedle's work.

Geiser said he thinks the two researchers did a good job. He does not agree with Bunin's criticisms of their work. He said he, like Freedle, wants more more research on why blacks and whites answer these questions differently, so that any unfair disadvantages for blacks can be removed.

He said he thought the College Board, in particular, should "get over the denial" of any merit to what Freedle has discovered. That may take a while. The College Board, after all, may be right that the SAT is unbiased.

But the new paper means more researchers are likely to go more deeply into what Freedle has found, and eventually settle the question of what should be done about it.

13

A Lack of Reading Causes African Americans to Fare Poorly on the SAT Test

Veda Jairrels

Veda Jairrels is a professor of exceptional education at Clark Atlanta University.

It is a fact that African-American students score lower than other groups on standardized tests. Among the factors that have a positive impact on test scores, the most significant is the amount of time a child is read to in the home. Overall, African Americans tend to read to their children less than any other group. Thus, African Americans can improve the scores of their children on standardized tests by simply reading more to them.

African American students, as a group, usually (not always) score the lowest on standardized tests. I believe African Americans score the lowest on standardized tests that focus on verbal (reading) ability because of a lack of "long-term voluntary reading". . . .

[Tom] Fischgrund conducted research that is relevant to this [viewpoint]. He studied 160 out of 541 students who made perfect scores on the SAT in 2000. The students completed questionnaires, and Fischgrund also interviewed some of them. At the time of his study, a perfect score was 1600. (Currently, with the recently added Writing Section, a perfect

Veda Jairrels, "Introduction: Why African Americans Usually Score the Lowest on Standardized Tests (Just Keeping It Real)," *African Americans and Standardized Tests: The Real Reason for Low Test Scores*, 2009, pages vii, 61 63, 72–80. Copyright © 2009 by African American Images, Inc. All rights reserved. Reproduced by permission.

score is 2400.) He also compared them to a group of test takers (the "control group") that scored from 1000 to 1200 in Critical Reading and Mathematics, which he said were average to slightly above average scores. It is important to keep in mind that for 2005 college bound seniors, when the score of 1000 based on 2 parts represented average, African American seniors averaged 864, 136 points below the average score of 1000. For 2007 college bound seniors, only upper income African Americans and those from well-educated families had mean scores slightly below average.

Based on his research, Fischgrund listed the seven secrets of those perfect score students. Reading, of course, was one of the seven secrets. In fact, Fischgrund described it as being "crucial" to success. The perfect score students' number one test-taking tip was to "read everything."

The perfect score students' number one test-taking tip was to "read everything."

What is particularly interesting is what Fischgrund found about the amount of time perfect score students spent reading versus the control group. Perfect score students spent an average of 9 hours a week reading for school and 5 hours a week reading for pleasure (not connected with school assignments) for a total of 14 hours per week. The control group averaged 4 hours a week reading for school assignments and 4 hours a week reading for pleasure for a total of 8 hours per week.

Therefore, the question for African Americans parents is, "How much time does your child spend reading each week? Does your child spend about 4 hours reading for pleasure each week?" Remember, for 2007 college bound African Americans seniors, the mean score was 1287, 213 points below the test midpoint of 1500. On the Critical Reading section, the African American mean for 2007 seniors was 433, 67 points lower than the designated test midpoint of 500. Therefore, approximately 8 hours of reading per week (4 for school assignments, 4 for pleasure) may be necessary, just to get the African American average (as a group) closer to the 1000 (two parts) or 1500 (three parts) mean.

Other Factors Affecting Scores

The issue of how much homework or amount of time spent reading for homework may also be a factor. Some educators have concluded from the research that the relationship between homework and academic achievement is stronger for older students but less evident for younger students. It has been suggested that students in kindergarten through the second grade should have 10 to 20 minutes of homework per day. For students in the third through sixth grades, the guideline is for 30 to 60 minutes per day and then for the seventh through twelfth grades, homework will vary depending on the subject.

Other characteristics about the perfect score students concerned their schools and family composition. Fischgrund found that 80% of the students attended public schools and 90% were from intact families.

There are others who contend that more reading equals better readers and that parents should read to their infants every day. Librarians have created programs designed to get parents to enroll their infants and toddlers in summer reading programs for the purpose of developing literacy skills. . . .

According to the Educational Testing Service, four factors can predict the average scores of entire states on the NAEP [National Assessment of Educational Progress] eighth-grade reading test: 1) the percentage of children in single parent households, 2) student absences, 3) hours spent watching television, and 4) children from birth through age 5 who are read to every day. When researchers used these factors to predict state scores, they came very close to the actual scores. They referred to the family as America's smallest school.

African Americans and Reading

There is evidence that some African Americans do not read to their children on a daily basis, beginning when their children are infants. According to the federal government, 68% of White children are read to every day, compared to 50% of African American children. The report also stated that children living with one parent are less likely to be read to than children living with two parents. This is a significant finding because in 2006, 35% of African American children lived with two married parents contrasted with 76% of White children. Children from families at or above the poverty line are more likely to be read to every day than children from families below the poverty line . . . 24.3% of African Americans live in poverty, and 50% of African American children in female-headed households lived in poverty in 2005. . . .

African American parents read less frequently to their children than White parents.

[Low]-income African American mothers were less likely to read daily to their children than were low-income White mothers, and this was not the only study to state this conclusion. Other studies have found similar results.

[Donald J.] Yarosz and [W. Steven] Barnett studied the frequency of parents reading to their children. The researchers analyzed data from the National Household Education Survey of 1995. The data were collected via telephone interviews with the parents and guardians of 7,566 children under the age of 6. The average age of the children was 2.1. The sample of children comprised 60.9% White, 13.5% African American, 20% Latino, and 5.6% were classified as other. The category of "other" consisted of Asian, Pacific Islanders, and Native Americans.

Regardless of their educational attainment, African American parents read less frequently to their children than White parents. Forty-seven percent of White families where the mother had less than a high school education, reported that their children were read to every day, which was the same percentage for African American families where the mothers had at least a college degree. In contrast, 69% of White families where the mother had at least a college degree reported reading to their children every day. In White families where the mother had at least a high school diploma, a greater percentage (56%) reported reading daily to their children than their African American counterparts (38%) and African American families where the mother had at least a college degree (47%).

Links Between Reading and Income

There is another study that is particularly relevant to the assertions in this book. In this study, researchers investigated the home environments of American children. They analyzed data from the National Longitudinal Survey of Youth (NLSY). The NLSY collected data through home observations and interviews. The results they reported may also help explain why low-income White students usually have higher mean scores on standardized tests than middle-income African Americans and why middle-income White students have higher mean scores than upper-income African Americans. Although they reported the data from several different aspects, I will focus on ethnicity and income. The researchers used the terms "poor" and "nonpoor" to refer to the socioeconomic status of the families.

The percentage of nonpoor African Americans reading at least three times a week was almost equal to the percentage of poor Whites but not equal to the percentage of nonpoor Whites. The NLSY also questioned mothers about the number of books in the home. A greater percentage of poor White mothers (41.8%) reported having 10 or more books in the home than nonpoor African American mothers (33%).

Again, more poor White mothers reported reading to their children at least three times a week than nonpoor African American mothers. The White nonpoor mothers also reported reading to their children more than their African American counterparts. A greater percentage of poor White mothers reported having 10 or more books in the home than African American mothers who were not poor.

Regarding children 10 to 14 years old, a greater percentage of African American mothers who were not poor had 10 or more books in the home than poor African American mothers. A greater percentage of poor White mothers, however, reported that they had 10 or more books than nonpoor African American mothers.

The researchers also found that the percentage of Asian American families reading at least three times a week or more to their children increased over time. Although White families were more likely to read to their children, "the dramatic increase among Asian Americans closed the gap by the time children went to school." The researchers did not divide the Asian American subjects into poor and nonpoor categories because they did not have enough poor Asian American mothers in the study.

[Ronald] Ferguson surveyed advantaged and disadvantaged elementary African American, Asian, Latino, and White students from mainly suburban school districts. Advantaged students were defined as those with at least two adults and a computer in the home. Disadvantaged students were defined as those who had a single parent and/or did not have a computer at home.

Ferguson found that the percentage of advantaged African American children who reported reading every day at home was not only less than advantaged students from the other ethnic groups, it was less than the number of disadvantaged students from the other ethnic groups as well. The number of disadvantaged African Americans who reported reading every day was the lowest of all the groups and socioeconomic classifications. . . .

These studies help explain why low-income White students have higher mean scores than middle-income African Americans. From birth, low-income White students may have more experience with the main skill (reading) of tests with a verbal focus than African Americans from higher income groups. White students from middle-income families may have more experience with reading than their middle-income African American counterparts, low-income White students, and low-income African American students. Low-income African American students have the least amount of experience with reading starting from birth and as a result, have the lowest mean scores.

Organizations to Contact

The editors have compiled the following list of organizations concerned with the issues debated in this book. The descriptions are derived from materials provided by the organizations. All have publications or information available for interested readers. The list was compiled on the date of publication of the present volume; information may change. Be aware that many organizations take several weeks or longer to respond to inquiries, so allow as much time as possible.

American Federation of Teachers (AFT)

555 New Jersey Ave. NW, Washington, DC 20001

(202) 879-4400

website: www.aft.org

The American Federation of Teachers was founded in 1916 to represent the economic, social, and professional interests of classroom teachers. AFT has more than three thousand local affiliates nationwide, forty-three state affiliates, and more than 1.5 million members. Among its publications are the newsletters *American Teacher*, *American Educator*, and the *PSRP Reporter*.

Carnegie Foundation for the Advancement of Teaching

51 Vista Lane, Stanford, CA 94305

(650) 566-5100 • fax: (650) 326-0278

website: www.carnegiefoundation.org

Established in 1905, the Carnegie Foundation for the Advancement of Teaching is an independent policy and research center whose mission is to improve teaching and learning. Its program areas include K-12, undergraduate, and graduate and professional education. The organization produces many publications, including *Organizing Schools for Improvement: Lessons from Chicago*.

The College Board
45 Columbus Ave., New York, NY 10023
(212) 713-8000
website: www.collegeboard.org

The College Board is a not-for-profit membership association whose mission is to connect students to college success and opportunity. It is composed of more than fifty-nine hundred schools, colleges, universities, and other educational organizations. It sells such standardized tests as the SAT, SAT Subject, PSAT, and Advanced Placement. Its publications include *The Official SAT Study Guide*, *College Handbook*, and *Book of Majors*.

Educational Testing Service (ETS)
Rosedale Rd., Princeton, NJ 08541
(609) 921-9000 • fax: (609) 734-5410
website: www.ets.org

The Educational Testing Service is a testing and assessment organization that develops, administers, and scores more than fifty million standardized tests annually in more than one hundred eighty countries. Among these standardized tests are the SAT, Graduate Record Exam (GRE), and Test of English as a Foreign Language (TOEFL).

The George Lucas Educational Foundation
PO Box 3494, San Rafael, CA 94912-3494
e-mail: info@edutopia.org
website: www.edutopia.org

The mission of the George Lucas Educational Foundation is to improve the K-12 learning process by documenting, disseminating, and advocating for innovative, replicable, and evidence-based strategies that prepare students to thrive in their future education, careers, and adult lives. The foundation conducts and publishes research, disseminates an e-newsletter, and makes a variety of information available on its website, Edutopia.

The National Center for Fair and Open Testing

PO Box 300204, Jamaica Plain, MA 02130
(617) 477-9792
website: www.fairtest.org

The National Center for Fair and Open Testing, also known as FairTest, is an organization that advocates for the reform of current standardized testing and assessment practices in education and employment. It publishes a regular electronic newsletter, the *Examiner*, plus a full catalog of materials on both K-12 and university testing to aid teachers, administrators, students, parents, and researchers.

National Council of Teachers of English (NCTE)

1111 W. Kenyon Rd., Urbana, IL 61801-1096
(800) 369-6283 • fax: (217) 328-9645
website: www.ncte.org

Founded in 1911, the National Council of Teachers of English promotes teaching, research, and student achievement in English at all levels of education. NCTE published the report *The Impact of the SAT and ACT Timed Writing Tests*, which raises serious concerns about the revised versions of the SAT and ACT tests.

National Education Association (NEA)

1201 16th St. NW, Washington, DC 20036-3290
(202) 833-4000 • fax: (202) 822-7974
website: www.nea.org

The National Education Association is a volunteer-based organization that represents 3.2 million public school teachers, university and college faculty members, college students training to be teachers, retired educators, and other education professionals. NEA's mission is to advocate for education professionals and to support the goal of public education to prepare every student to succeed in a diverse world. NEA publishes books, newsletters, e-newsletters, and magazines, including its flagship publication, *NEAToday Magazine*.

Public Agenda
6 East 39th St., 9th Floor, New York, NY   10016
(212) 686-6610 • fax: (212) 889-3461
website: www.publicagenda.com

Public Agenda is a nonpartisan organization that researches public opinion and produces informational materials on policy issues. Its reports on standardized testing include *Reality Check 2006: Is Support for Standards and Testing Fading?* and *Survey Finds Little Sign of Backlash Against Academic Standards or Standardized Tests.*

US Department of Education
400 Maryland Ave. SW, Washington, DC   20202
(800) 872-5327
website: www.ed.gov

The US Department of Education was created in 1980 by combining offices from several federal agencies. The department's mission is to promote student achievement and preparation for global competitiveness by fostering educational excellence and ensuring equal access. The department provides reports, facts and figures, and information about best practices on its website.

Bibliography

Books

Gerald W. Bracey *Education Hell: Rhetoric vs. Reality.* Alexandria, VA: Educational Research Service, 2009.

John Cronin et al. *The Proficiency Illusion.* Washington, DC: Thomas B. Fordham Institute and Northwest Evaluation Association, 2007.

Linda Darling-Hammond *The Flat World and Education: How America's Commitment to Equity Will Determine Our Future.* New York: Teachers College Press, 2010.

Daniel Koretz *Measuring Up: What Educational Testing Really Tells Us.* Cambridge, MA: Harvard University Press, 2008.

Jennifer McMurrer *Choices, Changes, and Challenges: Curriculum and Instruction in the NCLB Era.* Washington, DC: Center on Education Policy, 2007.

Linda Perlstein *Tested: One American School Struggles to Make the Grade.* New York: Henry Holt, 2007.

Richard Rothstein, Rebecca Jacobsen, and Tamara Wilder *Grading Education: Getting Accountability Right.* Washington, DC: Economic Policy Institute and Teachers College Press, 2008.

J. Michael Spector et al. *Learning and Instruction in the Digital Age: Making a Difference through Cognitive Approaches.* New York: Springer, 2010.

Matthew G. Springer, ed. *Performance Incentives: Their Growing Impact on American K-12 Education.* Washington, DC: Brookings Institution Press, 2009.

Herbert J. Walberg *Tests, Testing, and Genuine School Reform.* Washington, DC: Hoover Institution Press, 2011.

Periodicals and Internet Sources

Kam Wing Chan "Despite Recent Test Scores, China Is Not 'Eating Our Lunch,'" *The Seattle Times*, January 2, 2011.

Linda Darling-Hammond "Recognizing and Enhancing Teacher Effectiveness," *International Journal of Educational and Psychological Assessment*, December 2009.

Arne Duncan "Despite Cheating Scandals, Testing and Teaching Aren't at Odds," *The Washington Post*, July 19, 2011.

Susan Engel "Scientifically Tested Tests," *The New York Times*, September 19, 2010.

James Fallows "On Those 'Stunning' Shanghai Test Scores," *The Atlantic*, December 7, 2010.

Chester E. Finn Jr.	"A Sputnik Moment for U.S. Education," *The Wall Street Journal*, December 8, 2010.
Dan Fletcher	"Standardized Testing," *Time*, December 11, 2009.
Christopher Harper and Robert J. Vanderbei	"Two Professors Retake the SAT: Is It a Good Test?" *The Chronicle of Higher Education*, June 12, 2009.
Oliver Lewis	"The Gaokao Challenge: China's Fearsome University Entrance Exam Shows Us Why British Schools Are Falling Behind," *Spectator*, December 11, 2010.
National Association for College Admission Counseling	"Report of the Commission on the Use of Standardized Tests in Undergraduate Admission," September 2008. www.nacacnet.org.
Kristina Rizga	"What Standardized Tests Miss," *Mother Jones*, May 19, 2011.
Peter Z. Schochet and Hanley S. Chiang	"Error Rates in Measuring Teacher and School Performance Based on Student Test Score Gains," National Center for Education Evaluation and Regional Assistance, Institute of Education Sciences, and US Department of Education, July 2010. http://ies.ed.gov/ncee.

Sue Shellenbarger   "Education Reform and Leaving No Child Left Behind," *The Wall Street Journal*, March 25, 2010.

Bobby Ann Starnes   "Twisted NCLB or Twisting NCLB?" *Phi Delta Kappan*, December 2007.

John R. Tanner   "Incomplete Measures: In K-12 Accountability, Are We Answering the Wrong Questions Well and the Right Questions Poorly?" *School Administrator*, February 2010.

Phyllis Tashlik   "Changing the National Conversation on Assessment: A Consortium of New York Public High Schools Serves as a Model for a Multi-Dimensional System That Is Performance-Based," *Phi Delta Kappan*, March 2010.

Marcus Winters   "Costly, but Worth It," *The New York Times*, May 30, 2011.

Index

A

Accountability and standardized tests
  cheating issues, 70–72
  conflict over, 11
  curriculum concerns, 14–15
  NCLB and, 70
  in practice, 37
  research on, 75
  teachers and, 31–33, 42, 58, 71–72
  as useful, 27
Adequate Yearly Progress (AYP), 32
African American students
  low-income, 70
  reading skills of, 91–97
  SAT test discrimination against, 86–90
  SAT test scores of, 83, 91–97
American Board of Internal Medicine, 15–16
Arkansas' Curriculum Frameworks, 26
Arkansas standardized testing, 26–33
Asian Americans, 83
Atkinson, Richard C., 87
Atlanta Public Schools (APS), 64–72
Atlantic Monthly (magazine), 9, 88

B

Baker, Eva L., 52–63
Barnett, W. Steven, 94
Binary rating system, 44–45

Binet, Alfred, 7
Bireda, Saba, 69–72
Bishop, John, 14
Block scheduling systems, 56
Board on Testing and Assessment of the National Research Council of the National Academy of Sciences, 55
Bracey, Gerald, 11–12, 20–21
Buck, Stuart, 24–33
Bunin, Laurence, 87–88, 90
Bush, George W. (administration), 8

C

California High School Exit Exam (CAHSEE), 37
Caperton, Gaston, 78–80
Change.gov web site, 25
China, standardized testing, 7–10
Chinese National Higher Education Entrance Examinations (Gaokao), 7
Classroom practice observations, 61–62
College admissions, 12, 78–80
College Board, 7–8, 87, 89
College Entrance Examination Board, 7
College of the Holy Cross, 82–85
Common core standards, 42–43
Comprehensive Test of Basic Skills (CTBS), 22
Core concepts, understanding, 40–42